RHODE ISLAND COLONIAL GLEANINGS

The Records
of the
Proprietors
of the
Narragansett

Otherwise Called

THE FONES RECORD

James N. Arnold

HERITAGE BOOKS
2010

HERITAGE BOOKS
AN IMPRINT OF HERITAGE BOOKS, INC.

Books, CDs, and more—Worldwide

For our listing of thousands of titles see our website
at
www.HeritageBooks.com

A Facsimile Reprint
Published 2010 by
HERITAGE BOOKS, INC.
Publishing Division
100 Railroad Ave. #104
Westminster, Maryland 21157

Originally published:
Rhode Island
circa 1891

— Publisher's Notice —
In reprints such as this, it is often not possible to remove blemishes from the original. We feel the contents of this book warrant its reissue despite these blemishes and hope you will agree and read it with pleasure.

International Standard Book Numbers
Paperbound: 978-0-7884-2057-3
Clothbound: 978-0-7884-8542-8

Introductory Note.

The importance of the " Fones Records " require that they should be annotated, but the peculiar situation and condition of our State Records are such that the proper care and attention they deserve cannot now be given them. In order there fore that this record may have the attention it deserves, the compiler publishes them in their present form and intends to publish some time, in the future notes explanatory, historical and critical illustrating the matter here treated. He wishes therefore that all readers who have anything that will aid him or any suggestions or can refer him to any authorities that will be of service to him, to do so. The Narragansett History is of great interest to New England and it is the sincere wish of the compiler that all evidence bearing on the subject may come before him that he may be enabled to present in this work, this historical gem Rhode Island is so justly entitled too.

Introduction.

THE FONES RECORDS beyond all doubt, are the most historic Land Evidence compilation extant to day in New England. The fate of our state at one time depended upon the success or failure of the scheme recorded in this work. Samuel Cranston successfully overthrew the whole matter and to reward him the People of the State elected and re-elected him Governor until his death he serving them in this office near thirty years. If political fortunes were made ;

fortunes also were ruined by the exposure. In the whole it was a very severe lesson unto all engaged in it and a warning to these who have not learned the lesson, that even the best laid plans of men go often wrong.

In regard to the preservation in print of our Colonial Records both Town and State, our people have been very indifferent, not to say careless. Such an institution as a Historical Society we have in name only. What has been done in the line of historical and genealogical preservation has been undertaken and carried through entirely by independent sources. We know by our own personal experience that where we should have looked for encouragement, kindly advice, and friendly interest, we found our bitterest enemies and such that even went outside of truth to work us an injury. Our path, not over pleasant at the best, has been rendered very disagreeable by men whose extreme selfishness have given very narrow-minded conceptions of literary qualifications. While we have had many things unpleasant to contend against, we have also had things encourageing and peculiarly pleasant.

One of these pleasant features happened to us in January, 1891, when with the advice of friends we prepared a petition to the City Council of Providence to have the Early Records placed in print. Our petition was also signed by a number of scholarly and thoughtful gentlemen in full accord and sympathy with us in our laudable work and they aided us in our effort, This petition was favorably acted upon. The result was that a start was made and has been since continued until now, (March 1894,) the 5th volume is before us in print.

We have always had a pride in this matter that we accomplished the work with our friends, aid of started and putting into successful operation so desireable a work.

To show more fully the matter, we here publish the original papers.

To the Honorable, the City Council of the City of Providence:

The undersigned respectfully represents that it has become a matter of the utmost importance that steps be at an early day taken to preserve the early records of the town of Providence by printing the same after the general form and in the manner pursued by the city of Boston.

The undersigned having had large experience in deciphering and printing old records, would respectfully ask your Honorable Body to raise a special committee, who shall consider this matter; here your petitioner, in further explanation, examine the printed books of the Boston Records, which your petitioner will exhibit, and report to your Honorable Body the plan found most feasible for preserving our early records, which are of such inestimable value.

JAMES N. ARNOLD.

We, the undesigned citizens of the city of Providence hereby respectfully recommend the foregoing petition to your favorable consideration, fully recognizing the great importance thereof.

J. ERASTUS LESTER.
G. M. CARPENTER.
E. C. MOWRY.
C. H. GEORGE.
AMASA M. EATON.
E. BENJ. ANDREWS.
REUBEN A. GUILD.
HENRY R. BARKER.
J. O. AUSTIN.
GEO. T. HART.
CHARLES W. HOPKINS.

Presented by John E. Kendrick and referred to Committee on Education January 19, 1891.

(From Providence Journal and Bulletin Jan. 20, 1891.)

" Mr. John E. Kendrick presented the petition of G. M. Carpenter et al to preserve the early records of the town of Providence. Refered to the Committee on Education."

(January 19, 1891.)

IN COMMON COUNCIL.

Of G. A. Carpenter et al. relative to preserving the early records of the town of Providence. To the Committee on Education.

Read. Thereupon it is ordered that the same be received.

Passed in Common Council March 2, 1891. In Board of Aldermen March 5, 1891.

(Copy of Records of the Common Council March 2, 1891)

" Upon recommendation of the Committee on Education a resolution is read and passed appointing a Record Commission to and appropriating the sum of $1000. Therefore, the roll being call as follows: Ayes 36. Noes none, absent or not voting 4."

COMMITTEE ON EDUCATION.

John E. Kendrick, Chairman ; George E. Barstow, Edward S. Aldrich, John J. Gilmartin, Alderman Elisha Dyer.

No. 115. Report of the Joint Committee on Education Relative to Printing Old Town Records.

(Presented March 2, 1891.)

To the Honorable the City Council of the City of Providence :

The Joint Standing Committee of the City Council on Education, to whom was referred in Board of Aldermen, July 2, 1890, and in Common Council, January 19, 1891. petitions praying that the early records of the town may be printed, respectfully report :

That there are several ancient books of record in the offices of the City Clerk, of the Clerk of the Municipal Court and of the Recorder of Deeds, which are in such a condition, from long use, that the preservation of their valuable contents can be accomplished only by reproducing them in a substantial and permanent form. These records are highly valuable; first, as furnishing material for the very important and interesting early history of the town; and, secondly, as furnishing evidence by deeds, layouts, wills and many other particulars of the greatest consequence in tracing and proving the ownership and descent of property. In their present condition, they are in large part legible only by experts, and they are subject to the changes of destruction from wear and accident.

Your committee are of the opinion that these records should be reproduced by printing rather than by writing. The printed will be more legible, can be examined by several investigators at the same time, will not be subject to mischievous alteration, and the possession of a number of copies will enable the city to make to other Municipal Governments and to Public Libraries such distribution of these monumental records of our early history as may seem proper.

They have endeavored to ascertain approximately the cost of such printed copies, but they find that a careful examination of the record books must first be made in order to determine how many volumes require to be reproduced, and in what style it is best that they be printed. They therefore recommend that this work be begun by the appointment of a Commission, with authority to do the preliminary work, and produce one volume of copies in a manner worthy of the importance of the work. On the completion of this volume, the Commission will be able to report much more definitely than can be estimated, the probable extent and cost of the work, and the City Council can better decide when and how far it is advisable to continue.

The committee, therefore, recommend the passage of the accompanying resolution.

JOHN E. KENDRICK, Chairman.

No. 116. Resolution Appointing a Commission to Print the Old Town Records.

(Approved March 6, 1891.)

Resolved, That Horatio Rogers, George M. Carpenter and Edward Field are hereby appointed Record Commissioners, who shall serve without compensation, for the purpose of collecting and printing the early records of the town of Providence, and said Commissioners are hereby authorized to expend the sum of one thousand dollars for collecting and printing said records, said sum to be charged to the appropriation for printing.

In face of the above facts and to show how very small some minds can be when allowed by selfish motives to control, we call especial attention to the first report of the Record Commissioners where in the appendix, They show just how far the so called Rhode Island Historical Society had interested themselves in the matter. Our work was done nearly seven years after they utterly failed to do anything according to their own published report. Yet in spite of this published fact, one of the Record Commissioners has the face to write this in a published address, (see page 19 of the R. I. His. Quar. for April 1894.)

" It was not until this Society pressed the matter upon the attention of the City Council three years ago that municipal action was taken."

We pronounce this an unqualified falsehood for the reason above given.

Having been so successful in this matter we have become so bold as to Start our new serial of which Volume I is now before the reader. It is proposed to make the RHODE ISLAND COLONIAL GLEANINGS an invaluable work of reference to all Rhode Island Scholars. The Compiler has spent years of labor and intense study to perfect himself for his chosen life work. He has thoroughly equipped himself for his work but at the expense of wealth, for had he but have put the same time and energy into some other business pursuit he no doubt could have accumulated some wealth in his now the twentieth year of historical research. We are not writing this introduction for effect but to give an honest expression to what one has to encounter in this state who tries to do a much needed work. The coming generation will be more liberal and just to us and we intend to leave behind us a written statement about some things that will not be pleasant reading to certain parties alive to day.

If there is any short comings in this volume and its appearance is not every way satisfactory will the reader please to remember we have done the best we could with the means God and Man has placed at our disposal.

If the public and our friends will place more means and encouragement in our hands another volume will follow this. We have serveral volums of the serial in manuscript which will be printed as soon as means are given and pledged for such purpose.

It is not our intention to put fancy prices to any of our works. The price placed in our present one of $1.50 is higher perhaps than some of the others will be held so far as matter is concerned. In brief we shall put the price as low as possible consistent with successful publication.

The writer takes great pleasure in having successfully published his VITAL RECORD OF RHODE ISLAND 1636-1850. The town records of the five countries of the state are now in print making a total of nearly 3200 pages. He is willing to rest his fame upon this great work alone which he considers a monument to his industry and long and very patient research.

NOTE—: The Contents, General Index and Index to Places will be founded after the text in this work.

THE RECORDS OF THE

PROPRIETORS OF THE NARRAGANSETT,

OTHERWISE CALLED

THE FONES RECORD.

(1) Whereas, Mr. John Winthrop, Governor of Conecticut maj'r Humpfrey Aderton of Dorchester, withe Several other there friends haveing obtainede a gifte or giftes from the cheefe Sachem or Sachems of the Naragansets the grande deede of giftes beinge hereafter Recorded, and for our more comfortable and orderly carrying an end of al things, and that things may be seteled we jointly here Agreed this Several ordere we shal follow after the Records of these deeds th's 4 November 1659.

Know all men by these p'sents that I Cogineaquon Sagamore or Schem of Naraganset. In consideration of that greate love and affection, I doe have unto English men especially, mr. John Winthrop, Governor of Conecticut, Maj'r Humphrey Atherton of the Massachusets, Richard Smith, Senir, and Richard Smith, Junir, of Cocumcrosuck. Traders Leiftenent William Hudson of Boston, Amose Richenson of the same, Boston, and John Tinker of Nashuway, Trader, have Given and Granted and doe by these p'sents ffully; freely, voluntarily, Absolutely and Effectually

Give, Grante, confirme and make over unto my said friends one Tract of Land in my country called by the names of Wyapumscut, Mascacowage, Cocumscosuck, and such like, be it containing more or less, bounded by the brooke or River called Mascaekowage on the North East bye a brooke or River called Cocumscosuck on ye South West bye Common path or way betweene these on the North west or North bounds. And by sea or waters on the south, to have & to holde the said Tracte of Land, togeather with the privelidge of sumer feed for there cattel, making of hay in all meaddows Swamps and Lowe grounds, without the said bounds to the Northward to them, the said Governor Winthropp, Maj'r Atherton, Richard & Richard Smith, Leiftenent Hudson, Amose Richenson and John Tinker, theire and every of theire friends, their heires and Assignes, for ever, onely excepted the Lands in possession of and belonging already to Richard Smith, Sen'r, w'ch was his proper Right and is expressed by deede before this grante, to be to him, his heires and Assignes for ever, and a Neck of land called Potowomuck included in this said grant wch I doe Reserve for planteing ground for me and my friends until such time as we see cause to forsake it, or lay it down as alsoe the privilidge of fishing and gathering of clams and other shell fish, all other the p'mises from the said Rivers or Brooks, Mascuchowoge Cocumscusuck, Sea and Path, and other, the privilidges before mentioned, to be there owne proper use and uses, to injoy and improve as there owne proper Right and Interest from henseforth, for ever. And I, the said Cogineaquon by this my deede of gift caled and delivered, and possession of the said land given before the witnesses hereafter mentioned doe Ratifie and confirme the same, and doe premis the same to defend from all other persons laying claime to the same, dated this eleventh day of June, 1659. Seae'd and deld in the p'sense of Awasshouse, Indian.

REUBEV WILLIS, Interpreter.

JAMES SMITH,   WESTER SMITH.

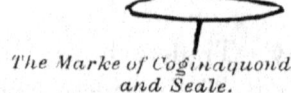

The Marke of Coginaquond, and Seale.

Note.—In the margin this is called "A coppie of the deed of gift for the north end tract of land." "Exam No. 1."

(2) Knowe all men by these presents, that I, Coginaquand, chiefe Sachem of Naraganset, In Consideration of the greate love and Eaffection, I doe beare unto Englishmen, Especially mr. John Winthropp, Governor of Conecticott, Maj'r Humphrey Atherton of Massachusets, Richard Smith, Senior, and Richard Smith, Junior, of Cocumscosuck, Traders, Leut. William Hudson of Boston, and Amos Richeson of Boston, aforesaid, and John Tinker of Nashuway, Trader, have given and granted, and doe by these presents ffully, freely, voluntarily, absolutely and effectually give, grant, confirme and make over unto my said friends one tract of Land in my countrie of Naraganset, called by name Namecocknecke, be it more or less Cocumseoset Wannuchecomecut, otherwise called Anochetucket, Pawsackaron, Wannalcheremocut, Mattatuxset, bounded by the Brooke called Cocumscoset on the North East, from hence running on a West line as farr as Anochetuckett River, And from thence on A West line to the North West of a Ponde called Pawcackaron, on the South West bounded by A River called Mattutuxsett and sea to the sea, or Petaquamscutt, bounded by the Sea or Water on the South East; to have and to hoald the said Tracte of land, to geather with the priviledge of Summer feed for there cattel, making of hay in all meadows, Swamps and low grounds, without the said Bounds to the Northwarde and North West; to them the said Governor Winthropp, Major Atherton Richard and Richard Smith, Left William Hudson, Amos Richeson and John Tinker, there and every of there friends, there heires and Assignes forever, onely excepted the lands in pesetion of and belonging already to Richard Smith, Sen'r Richard Smith Jun'r togeather with James Smith wch was there proper Right and is expressed by lease or grante before this grante, to be to them, there heires and Assignes forever; Alsoe except an necke formerly granted to Mr. Holding, All which Tract, Necke or Neckes fore mentioned, I the aforesaid

Coginaquond, doe give and make over all and Singular, this my foresaid Land, to these my foresaid friends, to have and to houlde to them, there heires and Assignes forever, with all manner of Rights & Titles and priviledges there unto belongeing, and due promise to defende the same from any manor of Chalenge or Claime what soe ever, And I the aforesaid Coginaquond by this my deede of gift, sealed and delivered before these witness here after mentioned, doe ratifie and confirme the same And doe promis the same to defende from all other persons laying claims to the same.

  Dated this fourth of July one thousand six hundred fiftie nine.
Signed Sealed and delivered
in the presence of us:—
Nathaniel Greene.
John Vial.
Tho. Stanton.   *The Marke of*
John Stanton.   *Coginaquond*
John arnishee.   *and a Seale.*
Receid this sixt of July 1659, of Major Humphrey Aderton and the rest of his friends, the some of seventy five pounds, in wampum peage with several other things, as a gratuity for certaine Lands given the said Majr Aderton & his friends, as may appear by the Several deeds of gift I say received by me.
Test   Coginaquond   his marke.
John Woodmansey.
Jno. Vial,

  Note.—In the margin this is called "A coppie of the deede of gift for the Southend tract of land. Coginaquonds tract. No. 2 exam.

 (**2**) At A meeting of mr. John Winthropp, major Humphrey Atherton, Mr. Richard Smith, Sen'r mr. Richard Smith junr, Leftenent William Hudson, mr. Amos Richison and mr. John Tinker, at the house of Edward Hutchinson, this 4 of november 1659 it was o.dered.

  We who are nominated in these two deeds of gift doe all

of us Joyntly accept of and give unto Cap. Edward Hutchinson, equal sheire and Interest with us whose names are in the deeds, as fully as if his names had been inserted in both the tracts of lande, he paying his sheire as we doe.

Edw. Hutchinson Share Granted.

We alsoe order and apointe, that the tracte of land to the Southward of mr. Smith's Traiding house, shal be and hereby is set aparte for farmes for mr. Winthropp, Major Aderton, Capt. Edward Hutchinson, Mr. Richard Smith Senr. Leift William Hudson, mr. Amos Richison, mr. Richard Smith Junr. and mr. John Tinker in Equal protions.

Southern Tract for farmes in equal shares.

We also order and set aparte the Northerne Tracte of land for a Plantation wch we intende into sixty shaires And to give out of the same to such men as shall be aproved of by us, such proportions as shal orderly be granted them and that what proportions is granted to any shal pay to us, towards our greate charge we have been at, twelve pense for every Acker is Alotted to them and alsoe who ever shal have any lande there shal from time to time and at all times, them and there heires and successors for ever, contribute to the maintenance of an able goodly orthodox minister.

Ye Northerne for Plantations.

We also doe hereby agree that major Atherton and Capt Edward Hutchinson, mr. Amos Richarson and Leiftenant William Hudson, or any three of them, shal have full power as A committe to Act in all matters that may concerne the settling the said plantation, as Admiting of Inhabitants and ordering all matters that may be for the good of the said plantation and promoting the orderly planting there of, for this yeare Ensueing and till other order be taken therein.

A Committee for Kings, Provinces of ye Plantation.

At A meeting of Maj'r Atherton, Edward Hutchinson, Leftenant Hudson & Amos Richison at ye house of Ewd. Hutchinson this 21 march 1660–61, It was ordered that whereas Maj'r Josias Winslow & Capt. Thomas Willitt they purchased mr. Jno. Tinkers Right in the two tracts of lande at Naragansets wch was granted from the Indian Sachems that major Winslow & Capt. Willit shal have each of them a shaire as our selves in the Northern tracte and shal have mr. Tinkers shaire betwixt them in the Southerne tracte & in al other purchases are equal with us & a farme also in the northerne tracte to make them equal p'portions in the whol grante.

Major Winslow and Capt. Willit to have a share.

It is alsoe ordered that mr. John Browne Senr. of Seacuncke haveing a grante from Tocomino a bought eight yeares since of certaine of the lands wch is within the Compass of our grante wch he gives up into the companie that he the said Mr. Browne shal be equal shaires wth our selves in the Northerne tracte of lande And alsoe is received in as ful as any of us in ye last margaige from the fouer Sachems & for the midle tract of lande mr. Browne is to have halfe mr. Richison p't in Namocock neck & mr. Browne & mr. Richison is to have betwixt them A farme in some place of the northern Tracte to make them equal p'portions in ye whole grante.

Mr. Browne to have 1-2 of Mr. Richison's Share, &c.

Note No. 3 Exam.

(4) Whereas Coginaquond hath given to mr. John Winthrop and maj'r Humpfrey Addeton & pairtners two parcels of lande lyeing in Naragansets Countrie as apers by two writings, one bearing daite ye eleventh of June 1659, the other the fourth of July 1659 as may more amply appeare now we Ceshequansh and Scuttup chiefe Sagamores or Sachems of Naragansets doe freely & Absolutely give and make over al our right and Interest in both the said purchases of lande to the said mr. John Winthrop & the rest of his friends acording to ye contents of the said writeings as witness our hands the fifth day of August 1659.

Scuttop's own Confirmation of the tracte.

the marke  of Scuttop.

Signed and delivered in the presents of of us:—
Valentine Whitman, Interpreter.
John Sassamon, Indian Interpreter.
Edward Hutchinson Sr.
The marke of Panatuk.

Indian.

John Sassaman's Testamony. John Sassaman Affirmed before the court that haveing published his name as a wittnes to the writeing wch in writeten was p'sent when Scuttop the Sagamore within mentioned signed and published his name by his marke to the same andthat he was an Interpretor did read the said within written to the said Scuttop before he signed it so as he wel understood what he did And was alsoe p'sent with Ceshequonsh the other cheife Segamore said unto Scuttup that what he did In Relation to the confirmation of lands by Coginaquand given to the Gentm within mentioned as in two other writeings may Appeare he did and would owne as donne by him selfe & further with not onely Ceshequansh in his haveing said that the lande within given was not the p'perty his as it was Scuttops and therefore what he did was good That this was Reaffirmed on the 24th 2 mo. 1660.

Attest Edw. Rawson, Recorder.

Whereas this fifth day of August 1659 there is a friendship agreed upon betwixt Majr Humfrey Addeton and the Sachems of Narragansets viz. Ceshequonsh, Cogiquand and Scuttop the said Major Humfrey Adderton p'mise that he will be a friende to the said Sachems in any thing he can that is just and the said Sachems doe ingaige them selves not to selle or Alienate, give or dispose of any lande in there Countrie to any p'sons what soe ever, whither English or Indians, with out the consent and Approbation of the said Majr Humpfrey Adderton but if they doe the same to be null and voide. In witness whereof we have Interchagably put to our hands the day and yeare above said.

In the p'sents of these witnesses:—
       The marke ⟍ of Scuttup.
Valentine Whitman, Interpretor.
Ed. Hutchinson Sr.

Note in the margin is this "friendship with ye Indians & there promis not to sell any lande with out major Adderton's consent"
No. 4 & 5 Exam.

The Sachems' confirmation of ye Tract of land yt Coginaquond granted. (5) Whereas Coginaquand hath given to mr. John Winthrop & majr Adderton & other there partners two parsels of lande lyeing in Naragansets Countrie as a prs. by two writeings under hand and seale, one bearing daite ye eleventh of June 1659, the other the fourth of July 1659, wch writeings we have seene & Each Interpreted to us the Domentions and grants in the several writeings apears now we Ceshequansh and Scuttup and Wequachanuit being alsoe chiefe Sagamores or Sachems of Naragansets and haveing with Coginaquand ful power to dispose of al the land in Naraganset Countrie doe freely, Absolutely & Effectually give and make over the said two tracts of lande to geather with the privilidges in the lande above it to the Northward and Westward, of mowing & feeding & timber of al our lande above the said lande up into the Countrie acording to the contents of the said writeings unto mr. John Winthrop Govn'r of Conecticat, Majr Humphrey Aderton of Massachusets, Capt Edward Hutchinson, Lieft William Hudson, mr. Amos Richison and mr. Richard Smith Senr. & mr. Richard Smith Junr. & such others as they shal take in with them & there heires & Assignes for ever. In witnes where of we have set to our hands & seales the fowerteenth day of June 1660 And hereby p'mis to defende the same from al others that shal lay claime

to any parte of the said lande from any p'sons of tital from
any others.

Signed Sealed and Delivered in the p'sence of
with three words or clause in the lost time after
the daite before sealinge and signeing.

John Cranston.
Caleb Carr.   marke
                                       Scuttup X his marke.

Valentine Whitman Interpretor   & a Seale
Thomas Minor.

Nucombe ye Indian. Sechequonsh his   marke

his marke.

                                        & a Seale

Awashus   Indian. Wequachanuit   his marke.

his marke.
                                        & a Seale

Quequashanuit's Receipt.

    Received by me, Quequashanuit, Alias Gideon A, chiefe
Sagamore of Naraganset, of Edward Hutchinson & William
Hudson, the sume of Eleven pounds in goods and peage at
eight a penny and is in lieu of what was promise from ye
last time we were at Naraganset for the confirmation of what
gifts Cogiquand had given formerly to us, & for the rest,
P'mise it is to be paid at ye Traideing house at Naraganset
wch eleven pounds work in peage at 8 A penny is in peage
at Six A penny the sume of fowerteene pounds, thirteene
shilings and fower pence I say received it by me this 26 July
1660 more paid five shillings eight pence peage eight A penny is peage Six a penny Seventeene shilings, six pense finial
is fifteene pounds, ten pence I say   £15--00--10d,

Witness   Quequacknuit

Christian Hooper
 1660

Robert the Indian ⅣⅣ his marke
 Interpretor.

Giddeon   his marke

No. 6 & 7 Exom.

*The Sachem's Mortgage
 of all there lands.*

(6)   Know al men by these p'sents that we, Suckquonsh, Nenograt, Scuttup and Wequackanuit Allis Giddion, cheife Sachems of the Naragansets, in behalfe of our selves & the rest of our Assotiates, doe hereby fully And Absolutely give grante and make over unto Maj'r Humphrey Aderton and the rest of his Assotiates and there heires & Assignes for ever al the lands in our countries comonly knowne & called by the name of Naraganset countrie, Neanticot Countrie & Cowesset countrie &c., excepting those lands formerly graned with in the said countrie, and are already publickly knowne to be Alienated by us, And doe hereby ingaige our selves, heires & successers, never to Alienate, selle, give or make over any pate of the said lande to any p'son or p'sons what so ever, but owne the said lands to be ye p'per Inheritans of maj'r Humphrey Aderton & his Assotiates, there heires and Assignes for ever, upon condition the said Maj'r Aderton & the rest of his Assotiates, shal clearely and Absolutely Aquit and discharge us, from an Ingaigement made by us, to the Comissioners of the united Colonies, for six hundred fathem of marchantable Wampum peage, to be paid by us with the charges arising thereupon, with in fower months after the daite of a certaine writeing, given Capt. George Denison and Thomas Stanton in behalfe of the said Comissioners for that ende, Alwayse provided that if within Six months after ye daite of this writeing, we shal wel & truly pay to the said Maj'r Aderton and his Assotiates, the ful quantitie of the said hundred fathem of good wel piped merchantable wompum Six peage, to geather with what is due for charges, then this

writeing to be voide and of noe effect, furthermore we in gaige our selves, heires & Successors, that neither we nor any of our Successors or Assotiates, shal at any time here after selle, give or dispose any lands to any p'son or p'sons what so ever, haveing to Maj'r Aderton & his Assotiates or there heires & Assignes, And if we or any of our Successors or Assotiates, shal at any time after this daite selle, give or dispose of any Lande with in our countries, to any p'son or p'sons what so ever, haveing to Maj'r Aderton and his Assotiates or there heires & Assignes, such saile, gift or disposal to be voide, And doe hereby acknowledg al our Lande to be forfited to ye said Maj'r Aderton and his Assotiates, And to be by this writeing firmely made, owne, given and granted to the said Maj'r Aderton and his Assotiates, there heires & Assignes forever; And doe hereby promis and binde ourselves, our heires & Successors to defende the same from any Claime, tital or Interest of any other what so ever, from the day of the daite of there ps'ents, In testimony here of we have hereunto put our marks and seales this thirteenth day of October, one thousand, Six hundred and Sixty.

Signed Sealed and Delivered in
the p'sents of these witneses,
and Scuttup Sealed and set his marke to
for Wequakonuit by order from him as
al the persons afirmed

Panatuk ✕ his marke

John ⌒ his marke   } Indian Witnesses

Indian Interpreter
Valentine Whitman   } English Witnesses & Interpreters

Ruben Willis ℛ his marke.

Suckquansk  his marke   & Seale

nenograt his  marke   & Seale

Scuthop 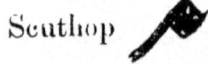   his marke & Seale

Scuthop alsoe maide this

marke 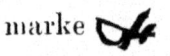   & Seale

in behalf of his brother
Wequakanuit & by his order.

   This deed is Recorded in ye 26 & 27 pages of the Judg Court book as attest Jno Allyn Sec'ty, Hartford Sept. 7 1664 No. 8 Exom.

(7) The names of such as are Assistants and have interest with Maj'r Humphrey Atherton in this writing and, have as ful Interest in it as the said Maj'r, paying there p'portions of what shall be paid to the Comissioners, In witnes whereof ye Maj'r hath put to his hande under this writeing this 13 October 1660.

Ye names of those that were interested in ye former motgage.

mr. John Winthrop Govener of Conecticat.
mr. Simon Brandstreet.
Maj'r General Daniel Denison of Ipswich.
Majr Josias Winslow of Marshfield.
Capt Thomas Willit of Rehoboth.
Capt Richard Lorde of Hartford in Conecticut.
Capt George Denison of Southertowne.
Capt Edward Hutchinson.
Leift William Hudson.   al of Boston.
mr. Amos Richison.
Elisha Hutchinson.
mr. Richard Smith Sen'r.
mr. Richard Smith Jun'r.   al of Naraganset.
Janas Smith.
mr. Thomas Stanton Sen'r.
mr. Thomas Stanton Jun'r.   of Southertowne.

mr. Increase Atherton of Dorchester.
mr. John Alcocke of Roxbury.
mr. John Browne Sen'r. of Secunke.

Humphrey Atherton
Whereas there is a writing upon the other leave of this pag given by Sackquansh Nenegrad & Scuttop in behalfe of themselves & there associates wherin they have made over al their lands to Maj'r Humpfrey Atherton and his Associates for the payment of Six hundred fathoms of peage wth ye *The promise to Maj'r Atherton aboute keeping ye lands in case of forfeiture of 5 or 6 years.* Charges to the Comissioners as alsoe an Ingagement not to selle any lande to any person or persons accept Maj'r Adherton & his associates suggest as more Amply apeares by the said writing. Now if this lande doe any waise come into the hands of the said Maj'r, his Associates or Assigns or there heirs or Assigns we p'mis to the said Maj'r and Agree amongst our selves not withstanding In regarde ye indians put a greate deale of trust in ye said Maj'r and expecte kindness from him, That we wil (not with standing) use ye Indians with all Curtesy and not take the lande from them for five or Six years, And when we shall have occasion to plante it that not with standing we wil suffer them to plant in the countrie & enjoy there priviliges of Royalties, And from time to time alow them competensy of planting grounde for them and there successors for ever.
Dated this 13 October 1660,
In witness where of we have Jojntly published our land.

 Humpfrey Atherton for himself and some,
 Edward Hutchinson for himself and some,
 Richard smith,
 Thomas Horton for himself and some,
 Richard Smith, Junr.,
 James Smith,
 William Hudson,
 Tho. Willet,
 John Alcock,

John Browne,
Amos Richison,
Josias Winslow,
John Sewett.

Note: margin marked No. 8, Exam.

(8) Know al men by these p'ents that we ye Sachems of ye Naragansets in consideration of five hundred ninety five fathoms of Wampon Required of us by the comissioners to be paid within four months, we say in consideration there of we doe freely, firmely morgadge, make over, bargaine & selle unto the Comissioners of the united Collonies all our whole Countrie with al our Rights and tightels there unto *Indians Mortgage to ye Commissioners.* and al the piviliges & Apartenances there unto, apertaining unto them, the Comissioners there heires, Administrators or Assigns, for ever to them & there proper use and behoofe alwaise p'vided that in caise we the said Naraganset Sachems shal wel & truly pay unto or cause to be paid the Governor of Coneticot five hundred ninety five fathoms of Wampon within fower months after the daite here of together with the charge of the five messengers sent unto us by the Comisioners that than this bargan Morgaige or saile shal be voide & of noe effect otherwise to stand in ful power & force in witnes where of we the Naraganset Sachems have here unto set our hands & seales this 29 of September, 1660.

Signed, Sealed and Delivered
in the pr'sence of us Quiscoquons ___+___ his marke.   Seale
Richard Smith,
Samuel Eldred his marke.

Seale.

Neneglad his marke.

Newcom, the Indian his marke

Scuttape his marke  Seale.

Awashous his marke

These are to testifie that I have received this 16th day of November, 1660, of Captaine Edward Hutchinson by the Apointment of Maj'r Humpfre Atherton and companie for and by the Apointment of Quescoquans & Neneglad & Scuttape, the three chiefe Sachems of Naraganset the full sume of *Mr. Winthrop's discharge of the Indian Mortgage.* Seven hundred and thirtie five fathom of Wampum peage whereof five hundred and ninety & five fathoms is for the much ordered 735 fatha by the Commissioners of the Collonies to be paid by the Naragansetts for some injuries and greate molestratuns to the English by some of their men, done at the new plantation neere to Manhegan, and at mr. Brewsters' farme, and the rest for the Charges of Diners messengers & others imployed in refrence to the same, we the said Sachems had alsoe ingaiged to satisfie and is in full discharge of that ingaigment made by them to the Comissioners under there hands and seales the 29th day of Sept., 1660. I say rec'd witnes my hand ye day of yeare above written.

JOHN WINTHROP.

No. 9 & 10 Exam.

(9) Be it knowne unto all men by these p'sents yt I Tumteckowe, chiefe Sachem of the great Pond and the Country there to adjoyning as alsoe of point Judea, Called by us Wenannateke being Eldest born of Webitamack Decesed wch was Eldest Brother to Ninicraft doe by these p'sents for and in Consideration of the greate love I beare unto Englishmen Espechally unto mr. John Winthrop of Conecticott Major Humphrey Atherton of Dorchester Capt Edward Hutchinson of Boston, Leift William Hudson and Amos Richinson of ye same Boston Capt Thomas Willitt of Wannamoysett Capt Jon Cranston and mr Jon Sanford of Roade Island,

Richard Smith Sen'r and Richard Smith Jun'r together with
James Smith of Naraganset have given & granted & doe by
these p'sents fully freely volintarily and absolutely and effectually give grant confirm & make over unto my said friends one
tract of land in my Countrie called Weyanicoke or point
Juda neck wth all ye Islands & necks adjoyning with in ye
ponds & so Eastward to pitt Comicutt harbor or Crick being
bounded on ye South East and South and Southwest by ye
mayne Sea wth said quantity of land be it more or less I ye
said Tumteckowe do make over to these my foresaid friends
to have and to hould the said tract of land together with sumer feede for ye cattel, making of hay in all meadows, low
grounds or Swamps with out ye said bounds of ye Northward
and Northwest of the foresaid neck to them the foresaid mr Jon
Winthrop, Major Atherton, Capt Edward Hutchinson, Lieft
William Hudson and Amos Richison, Capt Tho Willitt,
Cayt Jon Cranston, mr. Jon. Sanford, Richard Smith Sen'r
Richard Smith Jun'r together with James Smith
there and every of there friends, th ere heires and Assignes for
ever with out any maner chalange by me or in any name or
by my cause means or consent what so ever; And further I
Tumteckowe doe surrender up all Rights titells & paiviledges
what so ever to truste my foresaid friends forever to injoy
the same, And I the said Tumteckowe by this my deede of
gift Signed and delivered and po'sestion given of the aforesaid land doe Ratifie & confirme ye same and doe p'mis the
same to defend from all other p'sons laying claime to the same
dated this fonrth of march one thousand Siz hundred fifty
& nine.

          Tumteckowe   his
                     marke.

Signed & delivered in the
presence of

ye mark   O   of
     Awashous

Ruben   R   Williss. Interpretor.

his mark
Westen Smith
No. 11 Exam.

(10) Boston March 23, 1660.

Att a meeting of Capt. Tho. Willet, Edward Hutchinson *Northern Track to be laid out.* mr. Amos Richison & mr. Richard Smith Jun'r. It was Agreed that Edward Hutchinson should be Impowered & hereby is Impowered to layout the land in the Northern Tract of Land at Naraganset, appoynted for a plantation unto these Inhabitants of Rhode Island wch have a grante of Lands there unto such of them or the said which part provided they wil gi ve up all the writeings they have received from any of us Concerneing the same and give us a discharge upon the said writeings, that thereby we may have power of our selves to lay out as we see; cause the Remainder of the S'd Land And also the S'd Edward Hutchinson is Impowered to take a *Southen tract to be platted* platt of the Southerne neck, and also of the northern tract yt it may be Cappable of deeding.

Also to receive all Accounts. It is also ordered & Edward Hutchinson is Appoynted to Receive all Acounts from every of the partners of there disbursement & Charges as also to Receive of every person the Eighteen pence an acre of every man that have alotments & give acount to the Company.

The lots within to be built and settled in 2 years or forfit. Itt is also ordered that those yt have Alottments in the Town shall ingage to build upon them in two years space & to settle either them selves or some other upon ther lotts within two years time, upon the forfiture of of them lotts & if after they desier to sell them, they shal not sel them to any but such as the Company aproves of.

Maj. Atherton freed from Charge Itt is also agreed that Maj'r. Atherton (being a principal man amongst us, & one whoe we have cause upon Cause & ocasion to Respect) shal be freed from any Charge to the purchers & shal have his share with us of what is Received from any & upon the 18d per acre.

No. 12 Exam.

Committy. Wee whose names are hereunto subscribed, being appoynted a Comitty by the proprietors of certaine Lands lying in the Naragansets Country, wch Lands was given the S'd proprietors by the Chiefe sachems of Naragansets, in wch lands having Intentions to settle a plantation, & haveing Impowered us to Receive Inhabitants, & order matter accordingly. Wee the S'd Committy, haveing dully considered the estate of things, doe agree & determine That a certain tract of Land lyeing betwixt the Land of mr. Richard Smith Sen'r & to the Northward of him & unto a River or brooke, Comonly caled Stony River, along by ye English path & soe to Run into the sea. shal be divided into forty shares, twelve of wch *40 Shares Northerne Tract,* shares we Reserve to our owne, despose the other twenty eight shares, we give power unto Capt. Jno Cranston, mr. John Sanford, mr. Caleb Carr, mr. John Sails, mr. *p'sons to setle ye plantation.* John Green of Green, and mr. Jno. & mr. Tho. Gould, mr. Cuniegrande, mr. Howler & Valintine Whitman, or the Maj. part of them to take in such Inhabitants to them as they shal Judge sutable neibors to such a society, & hereby give them full power with our selves to act in all things wch Concerne the setteling of the S'd plantation & what ever Comouge it *Comouge.* obtaine from the Indians above the S'd tract of land up into the Countrey according unto ye breadth of the S'd Tract by the English path as also of the several shares & divisions of land within ye S'd tract wch is alotted to any that shal be Received in, as wel as to our selves & them we doe make over all our Right, title & Interest to them, and every of them, their heires & Assignes for ever. And we doe hereby promis to defend each others title against any yt shal lay any Claime to any *18 pence per acre.* part of the S'd Lands, they, the said partys paying to us Eighteen pence for every acre yt shal be alotted to any of them of the S'd twenty Eight shares, in Cattle, Corne or other good pay, after the Rate of peage at Eight per penny. In cause of or ocasion of the great Charge & Expense, we have been at to this day. And for what ever other Charges here after shall arise upon ye p'mises to be borne by the whole proprietors, that either is or shall be heer after Received from

time to time, dated this 15 June 1660.
A Copy of what given to ye above
named Capt. Cranston & the Rest Humphrey Atherton,
Ed. Hutchinson,
W. Hudson,
No. 13 Exam. Amos Richeson,
Rich. Smith Sen'r

(1 1) H. Atherton,
J. Browne,
R. Lord,
J. Alcock,
W. Hudson,
A. Richeson,
R. Smith,
E. Hutchinson,
S. Bradstreet,
D. Denison,
J. Winslow,
J. Winthrop,
T. Willet,
R. Smith,
J. Smith'
T. Stanton,
G. Denison,
T. Stanton, Jun.,
I. Atherton,
Ed. Hutchinson, Jun.

August 15, 1661.

Whereas upon 26 (5) 1661, there was a moeting of mr. Simon Bradstreet, Maj-Gen'l Humphrey Atherton, mr. Alcock, mr. Amos Richeson & Capt. Edward Hutchinson, it was there *A General meeting Appoynted.* agreed that there should be a meeting of all the proprieters that have Interest in the Morgage of the Naragansets lands, upon the 15 August next upon wch all the proprietors had Notice of it & those that did not appeare did desier, not with standing, there should be a meeting, &

they absent Ingaged them selves to be Included in what the Company did then & ther agree upon; upon a meeting upon the said 15 August of Maj'r Generel Humphrey Atherton, mr. Browne, Capt. Lord, mr. Alcock, Capt. Hudson, mr. Richison, mr. Rich. Smith Jun'r & Capt. Edward Hutchinson it *All the proprietors names.* was declared by Maj. Gen'l Atherton that mr. Bradstreet & Maj. Denison did consent to the meeting & was willing to be included in what the Company agreed upon, And mr. Alcock declared the like for Maj. Winslow, And Capt. Lord the like for mr. Winthrop & Capt. Willet, and mr. Rich Smith Jun'r the like for his ffather & brother James, mr. Stanton & Capt. Denison & Tho. Stanton Jun'r declares there consent by there letter, Maj. Atherton undertakes for his son *The whole Company.* & Edw. Hutchinson for his son, wch is the whole Company.

Impr. Edward Hutchinson was chosen and agreed upon to *Records* keep the Records of the S'd Compa. and to order them into a booke when voted & concluded on.

Maj. Gen'l Humphrey Atherton, mr. John Browne Sen'r, Capt. Edw. Hutchinson, mr. Rich. Smith Jun'r, Capt. Tho. *Committy* Willet, Capt. Rich. Lord, mr. Amos Richison or any four of them meeting together are Chosen a Comitty to act in the behalfe of the whole Company in the Naraganset business and hereby give them full power to act according to Instructions for one whole year ensueing;

first, that they labor to vindicate our Right, title & Interest *Instructions* ag't any person or p'sons whatsoever that shal produce any title or lay any claime to our Morgage land at Naraganset or any part thereof.

2. That they assist Ninigrat in making his address to ye Comissioners of the United Colonyes.

3. That they send Letters to mr. Winthrop to Informe him ye minde of the Company concerning ye matter of Jurisdiction.

4. They have power to call a meeting of the whole Company as ocasion shal Require, or consult wth any part of them

for advise.

5. What nesecery Charges the Comitty shal be at Concerning any business wch Concerns us, wee ingage our selves to pay our several proportions to them. These several Instructions was Consented to & Voted in ye Afirmitive by the whole Companie.
No. 14 Exam.

AUGUST 16 1661.

Major General Atherton's grant. At a meeting of Maj'r. Gen'l Atherton, mr. Browne, Capt. Hudson, Amos Richison, Rich. Smith Jun'r & Edw. Hutchinson, Granted to Maj. Gen'l Atherton a farme at the lower end of Namcock Neck of seven hundred Acres and the Rest to have there proportions of seven hundred Acres, a peice with in the Neck soe far as it will goe, and what wants to be made up out of the Land adjoyneing & what *Neck to be divided* any mans Land wants in quality, to be made up in quantity, he to make the fence wholly betwixt that and the Neck, And this seven hundred Acres to bee M'r. Atherton's whole share of that purchase.
No. 15 Exam.

(12) Whereas there is a parcele of Land in the Naraganset & Niantick Country, made over by the Sachems of these places to Maj'r Atherton and his Assistents of wch he hath *Sam'l Wilbere & other's possess themselves.* appoynted us, whose names are under writen to be of them, we paying our proportion of Charge that hath or hereafter shal be paid. And whereas we finde Sam'l Wilbere and others Indeavouring to possess them selves of our Lands, and wee, haveing prefered them either Tryal or Reference, but have no answer from them sent us. And yet further Indeavors by them to possess themselves further soe that wee cannot tell what they would have, or how far they intende to Proceede in there Injurious actings, Upon Consideration we Judg it our desires to take possession of the Lands by building and otherwise, We therefore doe in behalfe of *Order for building houses in Point Judia for the Company* our selves & the whole Companie Interested

therein, Impowere Edward Hutchinson & Capt. Will Hudson, booth or either of them, to goe to the Naraganset & Niantick Countreys and such men as we or they shall procure for to build what houses or to doe what else they shall think Conveniant about Petequamscet or poynt Juda or any other part of the said lands to tak possession thereof & in our Rights, and whatsoever Charge, trouble & Cost shal be laid out or Expended about the buildings or taking possession thereof, we Command & promis for us and heires, Execut'r and Administraters &c, to pay there proportionable Charge ther of with what else hath already been disbursed to the said *The Company Charged* Edward Hutchinson and Will Hudson and such other persons as shall or hath been Imployed therein for performance where of we binde us, our heires, Execut'r & Administrators &c by these p'sents. witnes our hands this third of December 1661.

No. 16 Exam.

Simon Bradstreet,
Dan. Denison,
Edw. Hutchinson, for my
selfe & son,
Will Hudson,
Ames Richison, for mr.
Winthrop & himselfe,
John Alcocke,
Timothy Mather, for my
selfe & my Brother in law
Mather for Maj. Atherton,
Jacovus Atherton,
Capt. Winthrop,
Wait. Winthrop,
Jno. Browne,
Rich. Lord,
Capt. Denison,
Tho. Stanton, Sen.,
Tho. Stanton, Jun.,
Capt. Hudson,

Mr. Richison,
Rich. Smith, Sen'r,
Ed. Hutchinson,
Mr. Richison,
declared to act for
Maj. Winslow,
& Capt. Wilcox,
mr. Alcock to
submit to within
ye Companis orders,
Ed. Hutchinson,
acts for his son Elisha,
Capt. Hudson, for
Jocovas Atherton,
mr. Smith, for his sons.
Tim. Mather, for
Rich. Smith, Jun.

Att a meeting upon publique Notis at Naraganset July 2, 1663.

Att a Meeting of the Company there mett the day above written, it was agreed to Send to mr. Tho. Gould, John Green & the Rest of the Inhabitants ther, to com to us to Consider of what Government to make Choyce of, whether Connecticott or the Island.

1. A Township to be Voted & agreed upon to be set out forthwith.

2 Whereas the Compa. have been at great Charge, for ther P'sent Recompense it is agreed to Reserve a place for 22 farmes, for ye twenty-two proprietors, of five hundred acres, each farme for the p'sent.

3 Whereas poynt Juda is with out harbor & soe for P'sent we Judg not improvable for farmes or plantation it is agreed, It is agreed that for P'sent it shal lye as Comon to the twenty-two proprietors for ther Drye Cattle, And also that ther shal be two houses built there, one at the goeing off of the neck at the sea, the other next petequamscott wch will be a Considera-

ble way to fence the Neck and this is to be don at the Charge of the Campa. & there shal be an Indeavor to get tenants for them booth. The two mr. Smiths is desired to take care to gett these houses built. mr. Amos Rickison is desired by the Company to goe to Conecticott to Receive an answer of the Letter sent thither in June Last.

all the above votes were voted in the affermitive.

No. 17 Exam.

(13) mr. Amos Richison, you are desired to goe to Connecticott and [inform them there has] been a letter sent by the Company of the Naraganset [proprietors to the] Council or Gen'l Court of Connecticott to desire the care of there [government for] more Comfutable proceeding, and what else according to what [was written] in the Letter were finding a proprietor a nessessity of Gov'rnm'nt, desire you to [get advise of] the Court if settling it not with the Council we may have a speedy answer of that Letter, and if they accept of us well and that good and [that] they appoynt forthwith some person that may be Impowered to grant writs of attachments & a Constable to serve them that we may be in on orderly way to serve any actions as we have ocasion against any & also yt disorder & profaineres may be supprest upon the place, dated 2 July 1663.

Ed Hutchinson by order of
the Compa.

No. 17 Exam.

Naraganset 3, July 1663.

We whose names are under written being the Inhabitants & the proprietors of the lands lying in the Naraganset have & doe desire (according to his Majesties grente) to be under the Govern'tt of Conecticot Collony & Request there protection according to a letter sent in June last.

mr. Bradstreet & others have desired
the same in ye Letter formerly Mentioned.

Richard Smith
Edw. Hutchinson and for his son Elisha

Henry **I** Tibit   Joshua Hawes   Will Hudson
his marke   his
     Sam **m** Eldred   Waite Winthrop
Sam **m** Waite   marke   George Denison
his marke   Jno Crabtree   James Browne
Alexand'r Al ffenick   ye marke of   Tho. Stanton Sen'r
     Tho. **S** Sewell   Timo Mather

    his
Sam'l **S** Eldred Junr,   Jno. Cole   Rich Smith Jun.

marke
     Ruben **R** Willis   Richard Lord
     his marke
Ambras **A** Leach   Ames Richisen
his marke
     Walter **H** House   Tho. Stonton Jun'r.
Enoch Plais   his marke   Increase Atherton

Georg **B** Palmer   Hen. Steavens   Rich Smith in behalfe
his marke   John Green   of 8 children
this was subscribed by these persons upon notis given to all
the Inhabitants to meet on this day all Subscribers that meet.
No 18 Exam.

June 16, Ano 1675.

Att a warning & general Meeting of the proprietors of the Southern Tract of the land at Naraganset in wch the Land Caled Boston Neck lyeth, it is by
the said Propriet'r Meeting agreed & Concluded in order to the division ther of viz ffirst That Capt. Edw. Hutchinson shall According to his desire have and Enjoy all his share & proportion of the S'd Southern tract of land Intire Adjoyning

Capt. Edw. Hutchinson his share to his farme already setteled. And that the line of his share of Boston Neck shal begin at the Mouth ther of, Runing from the Mill pond at the Narrowest place of the Neck, directly to the head of the Creeke neare his house at Lowe water marke, always Reserving to the use of the proprietors a Convenient highway to the water side betweene Capt. Hutchinson & Capt. Will Hudson's farmes, together with a Conveniant peace of land upon the water side for free landings or Wharfes in order to transportation of ye goods of the proprietors. That his Inside line of S'd share shal Run upon a direct line a Cross the S'd Neck & to have one hundred acres of land over & above his Equal proportion.

2ly. It was agreed that mr. Richard Smith shal have & *mr. Smith's share next to Maj. Atherton's* Injoy his share of land on the said Neck & also the share that was his fathers Next Adjoyning to the Land that was Maj. Hump'ry Atherton's at the south end of the said Neck.

(14) 3ly. Gove'r Winthrop shal have and Enjoy his part or [share of the said Southern tract to the north] to the *Gove'r Winthrop's share.* land mr. Smith's afore S'd.

4ly. It is also agreed as afores'd that Jno. Saffint & he *John Saffin's share* proprietors [that] the share of Capt. Tho. Willet wch Deed was Jno. Tinker's share shal lye next Adjourning to Gen'l Winthrop's land towards ye North.

5ly. Itt is further Agreed that Mr. Amos Richison shall *mr. Richison's Share.* have & Enjoy his share of S'd Neck next Adjourning to the Northerly line of Capt. Willet's Land afores'd.

6ly. Itt is likewise agreed by all & every the proprie-*Capt. Hudsons share.* tors afore said That Capt. Will Hudson shal have & Enjoy his share of S'd Neck betweene mr. Amos Richesen's share & Capt. Edw Hutchinson's South line.

7ly. It is further agreed by the said proprietors that mr. *Amos Richison s share.* Amos Richison shal have & Enjoy his Remaining part of the S'd southern tract Intire at & about Sugar lofe hill, &c.

8ly. It is agreed that all the Remainder or Surplusage of the s'd Southern tract shal be Exactly Measured & the outlines Run that each proprietor may know his due proportion.

No. 19 Exam.

June 17, Anno 1675.

The propriet'rs of the Northern & Southern Tracts of ye lands at Naraganset being this day againe mett have demand-
Payment for the farmes ed by them The said Capt. Edward Hutchinson, all the Money due unto them from mr. Tho. Gould, Robt. Spink and of several others of the Neighbourhood yt inhabit & dwell in these parts, of each one according to the proportion of Land he doth Legally possess & Enjoy at the Rate of Eighteen pence per acre, who did all that were then p'sent promise to pay each one his particular debt yt Remained yet Unpaid.

Thomas Nichols haveing fifty acres of land hath paid unto ye proprietrs his S'd purchas of Eighteen pense per acre by carrying ye chaine in measuring Land for Capt. Will Charles, *Nichols and ffowlers land* also by carrying ye chaine fur ye proprietrs hath paid for thirty-seven acres & a halfe of land now Enjoyed & possessed by Tho. Waterman.

Henry ffowler having one hundred and fifty acres of Land in ye S'd northern Tract, hath also paid mr. Rich Smith for the same at the rate of Eighteen pence per acre; wch land is now in possession of Hen. Tibbits. Capt. Jno. Cranston haveing three hundred acres of land now in the possession of Robt. Spinke, whoe hath this day past his bill for ye payment *Capt. Jno. Cranston land* of twenty-two pounds, ten shillings in Curant payment for the purchas of S'd Land at Eighteen pense per acre to Capt. Edw. Hutchinson Trusted to ye S'd proprietors

Itt is alsoa this day fully agreed & Mutually Concluded by all the proprietors (being then upon the place) that a certaine small neck or parcele of Land sittuate upon the water side or Creeke betweene the farme houses of Capt. Edw. Hutchinson & Capt. Wm. Hudson, begining at a lowe place on ye bank side Neare Unto Capt. Hudson's fence & soe Runes on a direct line a Cross the S'd small neck, against the middle part the top of a small knowle or hill at the head of the Little Creeke Runing into Capt. Hutchinson's Land; and from thence Runing on a direct Line down to th) water side, all wch Land bounded as afore said, (the little Cone of Medow within the said bounds only Excepted). which said Neck or small parcele of land shall be forthwith Equally divided into six shares or Equal parts for Each other proprietor, and for there future benefitt for Traffick & Transportation of goods & Merchandise. Itt is also at the same time Mutually agreed & fully Concluded [betweene the proprietors] That the line that Runs a Cross Boston

(15) Neck at the North End Next to Capt. Edward Hutchinson's farme shall begin at the Creeke side on the southerly side of S'd farme house at Crab Rock Neare a saven tree, on the bank side, & from thence shall Run directly a Cross S'd Rock to a Certaine poynt or small Ledge of Rocks at the head or Northerly End of the Mill pond, wch lyeth on the westerly side of the said Neck & is Near upon a northwest poynt, & is accounted the Narowest place of the Neck theire abouts.

It is also agreed on by the proprietors that Samll Eldred, Sen'r shall have & Enjoy one hundred acres of land, scittuate in some part of the southern tract with out Boston Neck, as soone as the S'd Land is laid out.

June 18, 1675.

Itt is this day also Mutually agreed on by the proprietors, that each of them, there Agents or Assignes, shall and will meet to gether at the house of mr. Richard Smith, at Naraganset, with mr. Elisha Hutchinson or some other sufficient surveior, or (in case he cannot be had) on the first Wednesday in Novem'r next, Insueing the date here of then to lay out & divide Each one his part & propotion of all the Surplage of the southern tract of the land of Naraganset, with all ye speed that may be, and on default there of then it shal & may be Lawfull and at the liberty of mr. Amos Richison, or his Assignes to bring up a Survaior & lay out for himselfe soe much land at or Neare Sugar lofe hill, as each proprietor hath for his part on Boston Neck, and when the whole of the s'd surplage is Equally knowne & layed out, the s'd mr. Richeson or Assignes shall, according to a due proportion Either Augment or lessen, & about the s'd quantity of land he shall soe lay out to make it Equal with the Rest of the proprietors, And for default by non appearanee of any one of the proprietors or Agents as aforesaid, he or they shall forfit & pay unto ye Propriet'rs the sume of five pounds in mony, And shal also confirme and acquiess & Rest satisfied in whatsoever the s'd proprietors or there Agents shall then doe & agree upon Except the disposal or grant of lands.

It is also by us the propriet's mutually agreed & fully Concluded that these our Agreements & all other of our Concessions shal be forthwith Recorded in our booke of Records of the lands of Naraganset in the hande & Custodie of Capt. Edward Hutchinson And that each proprietrs or other person Concerned may have recourse thereto and at his Reasonable Request have Copies thereof at there owne Charge. And for the full Confirmation of all & singular our Agreements, acts & Concessions we have here unto set our hands this Eight day of June, Ano. 1675.

No. 19 Exam.

        J. Winthrop.
        James Browne.
        Edw. Hutchinson Sen'r.
        Will Hudson.
        Rich Smith
        John Saffin.
        Amos Richardson.
        John Viall.

(16) In Boston, March 9, 1676.

Att a meeting of Sundry of the proprietors of ye Naragan-*Letter to Conneticott* set and Niantick Countrys it was then Agreed upon by the P'sons underwritten that a letter be written unto the

Goverm'tt of Coneticot to Assert our Interest there in behalfe of our selves & the Rest Concerned (& mr. Thomas Stanton being present did Consent there unto). & mr. John Saffin is apoynted as a messenger and voted to be impowered to act as an agent in behalfe of the whole Company as witness our hand the day & year above written.

The messenger

2. It is further agreed that mr. Thomas Deane be Treasurer to the Company to Receive mony of each proprietor according to his proportion as shall be agreed upon from time to time to defray the Charge in prosecuteinge.

The Treasurer

3. It is agreed upon that ten shillings be disbursed for a share at present.

Amount of Disbursetion

4. It is agreed That Elisha Hutchinson doe enter into the booke of Records belonging to ye Company, all agreements, writeings, Evidences & what may Concerne the Company from time to time till further order.

Enter on the Records

No. 20 Exam.
      Simon Bradstreet,
      Daniel Denison,
     { Waite Winthrop for three
       shares viz; my father's
     (Brother's & my selfe,

     { John Saffin for two shares
       1-2 in behalfe of ye heirs
     (of Capt. Willit & my selfe.

     Tho. Deane for 1-2 share,
  Elisha Hutchinson for two shares,
      Will Hudson.
  John Williams in the behalfe
  of ye heires of mr. John Alcock

In Boston, June 21th 1677.

Att A meeting this day of Sundry of the proprietors of the Naraganset Country &c. wee being the Maj. p't of p'prietors, viz. Simon Bradstreet Esq. for himselfe & Maj'r. Denison two shares; Capt. Waite Winthrop, for himself & Brother, three shares; mr. Simon Lynde for Capt. Denison, one share; mr. John Saffin for himselfe and mr. Tho. Deane, three shares; mr. Amos Richison one share, and Elisha Hutchinson two shares.

It was Agreed upon that Simon Bradstreet Esq., mr. Jno.
<small>Committy</small> Saffin & Elisha Hutchinson, (or any two of them with the advise of the other proprietors that are to be obtained in Boston), are and shal bee a Committy to act by word or writing in any the Concerns of ours at Naraganset untill further order from us or the Maj'r part of the propiietors of Naraganset above S'd.

Amos Richison   Simon Bradstreet for himself &
Elisha Hutchinson 2 shares.   Maj'r Denison.
Will Hudson; Waite Winthrop, for himselfe and his Brother.
Jno. Williams in behalfe   Simon Lynde.
of mr. Alcock's haires. John Saffin for himselfe & ye Interest
John Viall   of Capt. Tho. Willit's estate.
No. 21 Exam.

(17) In Boston August 5, 1679.

Att A meeting of Sundry propriet'rs of ye Northern & Southern Tract of Land in ye Naraganset Country: Viz. Capt. Waite Winthrop in the Right of Gov'r Winthrop; mr. Rich Wharton & mr. Will Taylor in P't of ye Right of Capt. Will Hudson; mr. Rich Smith for himselfe & with mr. Jno. Viall, in ye Right of mr. Rich Smith Sen'r; mr. ffrancis Brenly in ye Right Maj'r Hump. Atherton; mr. John Saffin in the Right of mr. John Tinker, & Elisha Hutchinson in ye Right of Capt. Edward Hutchinson.

It was Agreed & Acted.

<small>To write unto Mr. W^m. Harris in London</small> To write to mr. Will Harris in London that In case any shold Claime Right to the Naraganset or beg it of his Majesty, that then he wold maintaine our Right, & to Send S'd Harris twenty pound to defray Charges for the p'sent, & with him yt wee intend speedily to give him full power & further supply of mony.

Copy of Letter & bill Exchange are in mr. Wharton's or Saffins hand.
[No. 22 Exam.]
Dec. 8, 1679.

Whereas the Maj'r p't of the propret's of the Naraganset & Niantick Countrys &c. pertaining to Maj'r Athertons purchas & Mortgage Lands did sometime since Chose the Honble Symon Bradstreet Esq., Capt. Elisha Hutchinson & Jno. Saffin a Committy to Act in ther Concerns touching the p'mises & did also then Conclude that any two of the S'd p'sons with the Advise of the S'd propriet'rs in or about Boston, Shold at any time in Cases of greatest waight, Act in the behalfe of the S'd p'priet'rs & Conclude of all matters Respecting the Lands afore S'd. And, Whereas now the gentlemen of Rhode Isle that pretend title to the Lands at Petequamscott & some parte Adjacent have Chosen a Comitty to treat with us, the S'd p'priet'rs, for the Regular Settlement of the Extents and Limits of these our Lands, Wee the S'd pro- [*Agents or a Committy & ther power.*] prieters here unto subscribeing doe hereby Adde unto the S'd Elisha Hutchinson & Jno. Saffin, Capt. Richard Smith as our Agents & Comitty to meete & treate with the S'd Rhode Isle Agents for the Ends afore S'd. In Regards the Seson of the year is such that the Hon'ble Gov'r cannot attend the busi- ness. And accordingly wee doe by these p'sents Co'm·ssien- ate & Impower our S'd Comitty or any two of them together with there Agents of Petaquamscot Interest, & the proprie- tors thereof to settle & fully determine & sett the bounds, Ex- tent & Limitts of there & our S'd Lands. And In order here unto, wee, the S'd p'priet'rs doe hereby Authorize & fully Im- power our said Agent & Comitty, or any two of them as they shall see cause, by way of Compromise to accomodate & In- ·vest some worthy & meete p'sons with an Equal share & Inter- est In the Mortgage lands, together with our selves the p'priet- 'rs thereof, wch may tend to the more speedy Peopleing & Im- provement of these parts for the good of the whole & doe by the Agents for our selves, our heires & Executs hereby Ratti- fie & Absolutely Confirme and alow what soever our S'd Agents

or any two of them shall Lawfully doe or Conclude upon according to there best Judgements In and about the p'mises by virtue of this our power & Comition to be Irrevocable and
(18)   Authentick.
According to all true Interests & purposes of the Law in that Case provided. In Witness whereof wee have heer unto set o'r hands & seales this ffirst day of dec'br 1679.

James Browne   Simon Bradstreet for

Wm. Taylor  himselfe & Maj. Gene'l

Amos Richardson.   Dan Denison.

John Viall    Waite Winthrop for

                                  himselfe & Brother Winthrop

No. 23 Exam.   Wm. Hudso

                                  Simon Lynde, Attorney.

To Capt. Geor. Denison. ⎫
        Joshua Lamb.   ⎬
        Rich Wharton.   ⎭

Whereas There hath been for a long time Sundry diferen-
Agreement betweene our Comitty & the Petaquamscott Comitty ces Relateing to the propriety of the lands in the Naraganset, Coweset and Niantick Country, purchased of the Indian Sachems by Jno. Winthrop Esq., Late-Gov'r of Conecticott, Maj. Hump'r Atherton, late of Dorchest'r, deceased, & several others; as also purchases made by mr. Samuell Wilbore, deceased, Capt. Jno. Hull & several thers as by ye several deeds more fully appereth. As also

the Remaining p't of said Countrys, weh was by the S'd Sachems Mortgaged unto Maj. Hump'r Atherton & his Asotiates. Now for the full & f'inall determanation of all and singular the diferences that have been amongst & betweene the partyes above S'd or ther Successors. And for the better Settlement & accomodation of all p'sons and partyes therein Concerned. after many Indevors that have been used, WEE, the subscribers, by virtue of power given and granted unto Capt. Rich Smith, mr. Jno. Saffin & Elisha Hutchinson by the Maj. p't of that Compa. viz ; Maj. Atherton, & under hand and seale dated dec'r 1, 1679. And also by vertue of a power granted and given unto Capt. Jno. Hull, Maj. Peleg Sanford & mr. Josiah Arnold, by the Maj. p't of that Compa, Viz. mr. Samuel Wilbore, deceased, &c. under hand and seale dated like wise Dec'r 1, 1679, To Consider, Argree & Conclude of all Matters of diferences Relating to the S'd lands as by the several powers may now fully Appere, HAVE absolutely, fully and finally Agreed, determined & Concluded by & betweene each party & for our selves & every p'son we umpowering us and for our and every of there haires, Exec-It'rs & Administrat'rs for Ever as foloweth.

Imprimas, That those two tracts of land purchased by S'd Jno. Winthrop Esq., Maj'r Hump'ry Atherton &co., of Cojonaquant, by two severall deeds bearing date June 11 & July 4, 1659, & Confirmed by the Rest of the Sachems, shall be and Remaine unto the S'd Jno. Winthrop Esq., & Compa. ther Haires, Execut'rs, Administ'rs & Assignes, forever.

2. Secondly. That Samuell Wilbore, Capt. Jno. Hall & Compa. shall have a Certaine tract of Land, viz. all poynt Juda Neck, & from thence Northwarde up Mattatuxet or Petequamscot River to the head of the pond Called Pausacaco & thence

(19) upon a Northwest line Six miles, Also upon a West line (from the heade of the Cove North of Poynt Juda Neck) Six miles & a halfe, and soe a straight line from the head of the S'd Northwest Line unto the S'd West Line of Six

Miles & a halfe. And soe upon the same straight Line to the sea ; wch S'd Tract of Land is part of that wch was purchased by the S'd Sam'll Wilbore & Compa of Cojanaquant, Nenigrat, Wanamachon & several other Indians Sachems. This tract of Land according to ail the fore mentioned bounds with all these apourtenances p'veledges & Immunityes to be and Remaine for ever to the S'd Compa & to ther haires & Assignes & them only.

3. Thirdly. That the S'd Sam'll Wilbore, deceased, Capt. Jno. Hull & Compa shall from time to time & at all times hereafter & by these p'sents doe for Ever Quitt all Chalange, Claime, Right, Title & Interest what soe ever wch they or any of them have or had unto any & every part or parcele of Land In the S'd Naraganset, Niantick and Coweset Countrys Except what is in this Instrument Expressed to belong to S'd S'm Wilbore, Capt. Jno. Hull & Compa. wch s'd Land soe acquittes shall be and Remaine unto Jno. Winthrop Esq., Maj'r Hump'y Atherton, &c in part, and the other part unto the Mortgages, viz ; Maj. Hump'ry Atherton & Assotiates, there Haires & Assignes for Ever, with all its Rights, Members p'viledges & Appurtinances.

4. ffourthly. That Jno. Winthrop Esq. & Compa, Maj'r Humph'ry Atherton and Assotiates shall from time to time & at all times hereafter, and by these p'sents doe for Ever aquit all Chalange, Claime, Right, title & Interest, whatsoever, wch they or any of them have or had unto any and every part & parcele of Lands pertaining to the S'd Sam'll Wilbore & Compa as is above Expresst in the second Article.

5. ffifthly. That the Lands that are sould & laid out by the said S'm Wilbore & Compa to Jarad Bull & several other p'sons mentioned in that List, wch shal happen to bee without the Westerne side of the S'd tract of Lands, shall be alowed and made good unto them by the S'd Maj. Atherton Compa. AND, In case the North-west & West side of the S'd Tract of Land now Confirmed to S'd Sam'll Wilbore & Compa shall happen to Intrench upon or come within the lands Caled the Newbery plantation, the Centre whereof be-

ing at the Midle of the great Body of Medow & to be measured & Laid out six Miles square; then what part thereof as Shal come with in ther line & bounds afore S'd shall bee devoted and wholy granted to the S'd Plantation & townes use upon the same termes as the S'd Maj'r Hump'r Atherton's successors and their Associates shal alow; the Rest of the Lands to ye said towne, To and for the true performance of all & singular the Articles, Commands, Agreements & p'mises Concluded on by Each party Respectively each to other. Wee, the subscribers doe binde our selves & our Respective partners our & there Haires, Execut'rs and Administ'rs firmly by these p'sents. In Witness whereof wee have here unto set o'r hands & seales this ff r,t day of Dec'br, 1679, & in the 31th year of our soverain, Lord King Charles the second.

Signed, Seled & dell in p'sence
of us, Maj. Sanford being lame,
these subscribed:

Jno. Whipple Junr,   Jno. Dexter,   John. Crossman,

John Hull,    Richard Smith,

Peleg Sanford,   John Saffin,

Josiah Arnold, 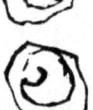   Elisha Hutchinson.

No. 24 Exam.

(20) On the Backide of the a ffore going agreement, is this written.

Dec'br, 5, 1679.

An acco't of lands laid out & allowed by mr. Sam'll Wilbore & Compa. to Jerad Bull, & several others wch the list Referred unto in ye within wretten Instrucment.

	acres		acres
Jereth Bull,	500	Stephen Northup,	120
Wm. Bundy,	200	Ambras Leach,	120
mr. Haveland,	400	Wm. Ayres,	120
mr. Low,	600	Widow Akins,	200

Hen Knowles,	500	Ben Congdon,	200
Jno. Tift,	500	a slip of land td Rouse Helme	
Tho' Fart,	500	betwixt him & a higway	50
Rouse Helmes,	200	Michel Casey,	300
Edward & Sampson,		Wm. Hefferland,	300
Sherman,	300	Georg & Ben Gardiner	400
Eber Sherman,	500	Will James,	200
for the Mill,	120	for the Ministry,	300
Rob't Hazard,	500	acres	2310
Capt. Alsbrough	500		5320
	5320	total acres	7632

Attested by us. The witnesses within named are
John Hull, Jno. Whipple Jun'r of Providence,
Peleg Sanford, Jno. Dexter, } of Taunton,
Josiah Arnold, Jno. Crossman, }
No. 24 Exam.

Dec'b'r. 5, 1679.

The Comitty Viz., Capt. Rich Smith, mr. Jno. Saffin and Elisha Hutchinson have granted four Equal shares of Land to be and Remaine unto wch p'son or p'sons (as the other Comitty viz., Capt. Jno. Hull, Maj. Peleg Sanford & mr. Josiah *number of shares of Mortgage lands* Arnold,) shall order out of or Equal with that Compa. Viz. Maj'r Hump'r Atherton & Assotiates. They paying ther several proportions of disburrse & charges.

Dec'b'r 5, 1679. The above S'd Comitty have granted & Confirmed (by this Voate & censent) unto mr. ffrancis Brenly one share or Equal p'portion of Land out of or Equal with that Compa. Viz. Maj'r Hump'y Atherton & Assotiates it being promised to him formerly by ye p'prietors———————

———————he paying his proportion of Charges &c.

Dec'b'r 5, 1679. The above S'd Comitty have granted & Confirmed, (by this there Voate) unto mr. Richard Wharton & unto mr. Will Taylor, each of them one Equal

share or p'portion of Land out of or Equal with yt Compa.
viz., Maj'r Hump'ry Atherton & Assotiates in Mortgage Land
they paying ther several proportions of disburse & Charges.

The line & two peices were Traced out in the p'sence of the
S'd Comittee & Company p'sent wch was don at the time
abovesaid & by their order therefore the vote passed.
Exam. & allowed.

(21)   In Boston, Octo'r 11, 1683.

Att a meeting of Georg Monks p'sent mr. Symon Linde
for the Interest of Capt. Georg Denison, mr. ffranci's Brenly,
Capt. Elisha Hutchinson for ye Interest of Capt. Edw. Hutchinson & himselfe, mr. Sam'll Sewal for ye Interest of Capt
Jno. Hull in Petyquamscott Land, mr. Richard Wharton for
his owne & mr. Wm. Taylors Interest, mr. Joshua Lamb for
ye Interest of mr. Jno. Alcock To Consider of wages to prosecute & defray the Charge of the Narragansett affaire upon ye
Report of his Majes'ties Com'isioners now to be transmitted
for England.

It was proposed by Capt. Hutchinson & Richard Wharton
proposal to raise money to the rest p'sent that whoever would Advance
& Adventure Mony for the occasion shold upon the Kings
Confirmation of the Mortgage Lands, to the Mortagees &
p'sons deriveing from them should have for every shilling
two, paid unto them or else an acre out of the Mortgage
Lands for every shilling advanced, But all p'sent Refused,
therfore it was Concluded & agreed that the p'sons p'sent
And mr. Wate Winthrop, Jno Russell Esq, mr. Richard Smith
How money is raised to send for England & mr. Jno. Saffin, should each Advance &
adventure uppon the acc't of the Mortgage twelve pounds in
New England Mony to be Invested into proper Returnes for
England to be transmitted & disbursed in the hands of mr.
Tho. Deane and by him to be dispended to the p'son appoynt-
ed to sollicitt said affaire or such other solicit'rs as may be
Employed as he shall see occasion, & Receive their accounts
Remitted to mr. Deane. of their disbursements from time to time. And that

mr. Deane shold be wrote to that if he saw a probabillity to efect there business, he shold have what mony more might be Needfull transmitted upon his advice not Exceeding one hundred pounds.

Itt was also agreed upon that demand be made of all the Mortgages to Contribute, & bring in the same proportion of mony *mortgagers to send in 12 £ a peice to Capt Hutchinson* for defraying former & future Charge, & if any Refuse or make unreasonable delay his share according to the first proposall & agreement of Maj'r Atherton with his assotiates to be forfited or to be disposed for the ende afores'd, the Mony aforesaid to be paid to Capt. Hutchinson.

It is further Concluded to write to my Lord Culpeper to *To my Lord Culpeper* acknowledg his former & crave his future favor & furtherance of this affaire.

No. 25, Exam.

Boston, March 21, 1683.

Att a Meeting at the House of the Hon'ed Gov. Simon Bradstreet Esq. were p'sent.

Simon Bradstreet	1	in his owne Right
Capt. Waite Winthrop	3	Gov. Winthrop Maj. e'lisha Winthrop Wate Winthrop
mr. Simon Lynde	1	Capt. George Denison
mr Jno. Saffin	4	Maj. Josia Winslow Capt Tho. Willitt Maj. Atherton Increese Atherton
mr. Jno. Alcock *appeare for the Interest of*	1	Doct. Jno. Alcock
Elisha Hutchinson	2	Capt. Edw. Hutchinson Elisha Hutchinson
mr. Rich Wharton	3	mr. Will Taylor mr. Rich Wharton mr. Wm. Wharton wch he is to have when Business efected.
mr. Rich. Smith,	3	mr. Rich. Smith, Sen'r. mr. Rich. Smith, Jun'r. mr. James Smith.

(**18**) Agreed as followeth:

Whereas, by a vote of the proprietors of the Naraganset Lands ther was on ye 21th of June, 1677; appoynted a Comittee (viz., Simon Bradstreet, Esq., mr. Jno. Saffin & Elisha Hutchinson) to act in there Concernes And the Weighty affaires of ye Hon. Gov'r Simon Bradstreet, Esq., presenting his freequent on that affair, We hare p'sent being ye Maj'r p't of the proprietors of above s'd Naraganset Lands have made Choyce of mr. Rich Wharton who is agreed unto mr. Jno. Saffin & Elisha Hutchinson, wch last three p'sons mentioned (or any two of them with the Consent of such proprietors as are at any time met together in Boston after haveing Notis given them that live in Boston), are and shal be a Com ittee to act in any of our Concernes Refering to & Naraganset Lands untill further order from us or the Maj'r p't of ye p'prietors of above S'd Naraganset.

No. 26 Exam.

	Jno. Alcock 1.	S. Bradstreete 1.
also was p'sent	Elisha Hutchinson 2	Wait Winthrop 3.
R. Smith 3.	R. Wharton 3.	Simon Lynde 1.
		Jno. Saffin 4.

(**22**) Att A Meeting of the Claimers & proprietors of the Southerne Tract (Comonly Caled the Neck purchas) at the House of mr. Richard Smith at Naraganset, April. 23, 1685. It was agreed as followeth:

Whereas, John Winthrop, Esq., Governor of Conecticott Maj'r Hump'y Atherton of Massachusets, Rich. Smith, Sen'r., Rich. Smith, Jun'r., of Cocumsessuch, Wm. Hudson & Amos Richeson of Boston, & John Tinker of Nashua, Purchased of Cojuaquand Sachem of Naraganset a tract or parcle of Land in the Naragaset Country, asp er deed, dated July 4, 1659, being bounded by Cocumsessuch brooke on the North East, from thence Runing on a West Line until the pond Lying at the head of Matatucket or Petequamscat River (wch pond is caled Pasacaco pond) bears *South East*, from thence South East, on the South West bounded by Matatucket River & so to the sea, And bounded by the sea or water on the south East. The above S'd Purchasers admitted Capt. Edward Hutchinson, Late of Boston, an Equal sharer or purchaser with them in s'd grant or tract of Land as appeares by theire Record. Namecock Neck being part of S'd grant was surveyed about twenty five years since & agreed to be divided into Eight shares, viz. seven hundred acres at the Lower end of S'd Neck, next the sea unto Maj. Atherton, wch he accepted of as his full share in S'd whole tract of Land bounded as above S'd. And the Rest of S'd Neck to be divided into seven Equal shares unto the above S'd proprietors, Maj'r Atherton ouly Excepted. wch S'd Neck was divided as by a platt under mr. Will Withington's hand in the year 1675, the order of Lying & the quantity of Land being laid & Consented to Remaine to the above S'd proprietors & such as appeare for them & on their behalfe; wch Land is to Remaine to S'd Purchasers, theire haires & Assignes forever.

The Remainder of S'd tract or purches being now Survayed & mesured by mr. John Gore, also mr. Rich Smith, land included in S'd deed taken into the platt, not with standing it Expresseth a West line to Run from the top of a Rock southward of his house, its agreed & Consented to by S'd mr. Smith that that line is to Run south forty-two degrees West to Annocatucket River, And all other divisions with mr. Smith's land above S'd to lye be & to Remaine to the several purchasers their Leires Executors & Assignes for ever as in the plat above s'd now taken & to be Returned to us by s'd Gov'r as also one hundred & fifty acres to Sam'll Eldred Sen'r fifty acres to Sam'll Eldred Jun'r, to them theire heires & assignes for ever the whole tract or purchas of Land contained in the above S'd two platts, as also mr. Smith's land included in S'd deed is to be & Remaine to S'd Smith with the above S'd proprietors or asignes, & Sam'll Eldred Sen'r & Sam'll Eldred Jun'r and to their Respective Haires & Assignes for

Ever in the same order for place & quantity & quality as is Exprest in the above S'd platts, And that each proprietor shal allow good & sufficient Highwayes to be laid out through their Respective divisions as heer after shal be by the proprietors, thought meet, Conveniant & Com'odius for the publique benefit & least predjuditial to any perticular person, In Witnes where of the Subscribers being proprieters or Claimers, in the Right of the above S'd purchasers have here unto put our hand & seale.this 23 d, April 1685.

Witness:

Richard Speare. John Saffin. J. Winthrop.

John Gore. R'd Wharton. Elisha Hutchinson.

Daniel Eldred. Asaph Elliott.

Alexander Huling. Rich'd Smith.

No. 27 Exam.

---

(23) To ALL CHRISTIAN PEOPLE to whome these pr'sents shall come, I Edward Hutchinson of Boston, in the Massa-
Hutchinson to Hutchinson chusetts Colony, in New England, send greeting.

KNOW YE that I, the s'd Edward Hutchinson, for in consideration of one hundred and fifty acres of Land I received of my Son, Elisha Hutchinson of Boston afores'd, which he gave a deed of unto my son in law, Sam'll Dyre, by my appointment, which Land is in the Narraganset Country, and is part of that he now dwells on. And also in consideration of that love and affection I beare to my son, Elisha Hutchinson, and other causes and considerations, me, at this present, especially moveing the receipt of which Land I do hereby acknowledge, and my Selfe there with fully satisfied and paid and of every part and parcel thereof do cleerly acquit, exonorate and discharge the s'd Elisha Hutchinson, his heires, Execut'rs & Adm'rs forever, by these presents HATH given, granted, bargained sold, aliened, enfeaffed and confirmed and doth by these presents give, grant, bargain, sell, alien, enfeaffe and confirme unto the said Elisha Hutchinson, his heires, Executors, Adm'rs and asignes forever all that the one halfe of a Farme or parcel of Land, the content of the whole ffarme is about One thousand acres lying & being in the Naraganset Country, on a Neck of Land commonly called Boston Neck, and is Joyning to the Land of Capt. William Hudson, and is in the occupation of John Cole, which Land is to be divided for quantity and quality, equally in all respects, with one halfe of all its meadows, feedings, woods, wages, commons & appurtenances whatsoever to it belonging or any wise appertaining TO HAVE & TO HOLD all and singular the before hereby bargained premises, granted and sold or herein mentioned to be granted, bargained and sold to the S'd Elisha Hutchinson, his heires. Exec'rs, Adm'rs and assignes To the onely proper use & behoofe of the said Elisha Hutchinson, his heires, Exec'rs, Adm'rs and assignes for ever. And I, the s'd Edward Hutchinson, for me, my Exec'rs and Adm'rs do covenant promis and grant to, and with the s'd Elisha Hutchinson, his Exec'rs, Adm'rs & assignes by these presents in manner and forme as followeth (that is to say) That I, the s'd Edward Hutchinson, at the time of the Ensealing and delivery of these presents am the true, sole and onely lawful Owner, possessor and proprietor of the before hereby granted premises, and every part and parcel thereof. And that I, the s'd Edward Hutchinson, of my Selfe have full power and lawfull Authority to bargain, sell, give, grant and confirme the afores'd premises unto the said Elisha Hutchinson, his Exec'rs, Adm'rs and assignes to his and their own proper use and behoofe for ever, according to the tenor and true meaning of these presents. AND that I, the s'd Edward Hutchinson, my Exec'rs and Adm'rs shall & will, from time to time, and at all times, hereafter cleerly and lawfully discharge and acquit, or other wise sufficient save harmless as well the before hereby granted and bargained premises, and every part and parcel thereof. As also the S'd Elisha Hutchinson, his Exec'rs, Adm'rs and assignes, and every of them of and from all and singular former bargains, sales, mortgages, gifts, grants, molestations, titles and incumbrances whatsoever, had made, done, or occasioned to be done by, from or under me, the s'd Edward Hutchinson, before the Ensealing and delivery hereof. AND that the s'd Elisha Hutchinson, his Exec'rs, Adm'rs and assignes shall or lawfully may, from time to time, and at all times hereafter peacefully and quietly have, hold, enjoy and dispose of the said before granted and bargained premises without the let, trouble, molestation,

(24) or Sute of me, the s'd Edward Hutchinson, my Exec'rs, Adm'rs or any other person or persons whatsoever from by or under me. AND that I, the s'd Edward Hutchinson, my Exec'rs & Adm'rs, shall and will warrant and defend the before granted, bargained premises, and every part and parcel thereof against all people, from, by or under me, to the said Elisha Hutchinson, his Exec'rs, Adm'rs and assignes forever to the use in the manner and forme afores'd for ever by these presents. AND the S'd Edward Hutchinson doth further covenant & promiss with and unto the S'd Elisha Hutchinson, his heires and assignes That (if occasion so require) he, the s'd Edward Hutchinson, will at any time hereafter, upon the reasonable request of the s'd Elisha Hutchinson, his heirs or assignes give what further assurance or assurances as shall or may be requisite or necessary for the making this deed Valid in law, according to the true intent & meaning thereof, whither by acknowledgeing these presents before Authority or otherwise. In Testimony whereof I, the S'd Edward Hutchinson, to these presents have set to my hand & seale this twenty third day of March, In the yeare of our Lord, One thousand six

hundred Seventy two, 1671–72.

Edward Hutchinson (a Seale on a table).
Signed, Sealed and Deliv'd.
John Usher, Wm. Hutchinson.

John Usher, Esq., above subscribed, made oath before the subscribers, one of the Council of his Ma'ties Territory in New England, That being present at the time he saw Edward Hutchinson within written, Subscribe Seale and owne the within Instrument, delivering it as his act and deed. This done in Boston ye 16th day of June, 1686.

John Pynchon.
No. 28 Exam.

To ALL PE)PLE unto whome these presents shall come: Jona-
Atherton to Saffin & Co. than Atherton, son and heire to Major Humphrey Atherton, sometime of Dorchester, in New England, dec'd haveing also had Administracon granted upon the estate of his s'd ffather, sendeth greeting: KNOW YE that I, the S'd Jonathan Atherton, for and in consideration of the sume of ffourteen pounds current money of New England to me in hand paid before the Ensealing & delivery of these presents by John Saffin and Thomas Deane of Boston, in New England afore-s'd, Merchants, the receipt whereof I do acknowledge by these presents, and myselfe therewith fully paid and satisfied, HAVE given, granted, bargained and sold, and by these presents do freely, fully and absolutely give, grant, bargain, sell, alien, enfeoffe and confirme unto the s'd John Saffin and Thomas Deane in equal halves and proportion all that my part and proportion of all and singular the Lands lying & being in the Narraganset Country & Countrys adjacent, which were formerly mortgaged by the Indian Sachems unto my S'd deceased Father and his Associates (which Lands are since forfited and possession thereof given, as by the S'd mortgage, bearing date the thirteenth day of October, 1660, and

other Evidences and writings relating thereunto, may and doth appeare) being the whole right, title and interest in the s'd Land that did belong unto my s'd ffather, and now right fully descended and in all respects legally appertaining unto me as his lawful heire.

(25) To HAVE AND TO HOLD the above granted Lands with all & singular the rights, liberties, privileges, emoluments and appurtenances belonging unto the same, or any part or parcel thereof, with all deeds, writings and evidences whatsoever touching or concerning the same unto them, the said John Saffin and Thomas Deane, their heires and assignes, and to their onely proper use, benefit and behoofe for ever in equall halves & proportion as afore s'd. AND I, the s'd Jonathan Atherton, for my selfe, my heires, Exec'rs and Adm'rs do hereby covenant and grant to and with the S'd John Saffin and Thomas Deane, their heires and assignes, That at the time of this bargain and sale, and before the Ensealing and delivery of these presents, I was the true, sole and lawfull Owner of the above granted Lands, and stand Lawfully seized and possessed of the same in my own proper right of a good perfect and absolute Estate of inheritance in fee simple, and had in my selfe full power and lawfull Authority the same to grant, bargain, sell, convey and assure the same as above s'd, And shall and will warrant and defend forever the above granted premises, and every part and parcel thereof unto them, the s'd John Saffin and Thomas Deane, their heires and assignes against all and every person and persons whatsoever haveing, claiming or pretending to have or claim any legal right, title or interest of in or to the same by any waise or meanes whatever. AND that I, the said Jonathan Atherton, shall and will at all times hereafter (upon request made to me for that end) do and performe all such further act or acts, thing or things, whither by acknowledging this present deed or by giveing such further and ample assurance of all the afore bargained premisses for the futher confirmation thereof unto the S'd Saffin and Deane, their

heires and assignes, as in law or equity can be desired or required.

IN WITNESS whereof I, the s'd Jonathan Atherton, have hereunto put my hand and seale this thirteenth day of ffebruary, In the twenty ninth year of the Reign of our Sovereign Lorde, King Charles the second.

Jonathan Atherton.

Locus Sigilli.

Anno qu Dom, 1676-7.

Signed, Sealed and Deliv'rd
in presence of us,

Isa. Addington. Bernard Trott,
John Pole.

This Instrement was acknowledged the 13th ffeb'ry, 1676-6, Before John Leverett, Gov'r.

No. 29 Exam.

To ALL PEOPLE unto whome these presents shall come: Jonathan Atherton, now resident in Boston, in New England, marrin'r, sendeth greeting: KNOW YE that I, the s'd Jonathan Atherton, as son and right heire of maj'r Humphrey Atherton, late of Dorchester, in New England, dec'd. and also as Administrator of the Estate of Increase Atherton, younger son of the S'd Humphrey Atherton, dec'd, for and in consideration of a voluable sume of lawfull money of New England to me in hand paid before the Ensealing and delivery of these presents by John Saffin of Boston afores'd, merch't, the receipt whereof I do hereby acknowledge, and my selfe therewith full paid and satisfied, Have given, granted, bargained and sold, and by these presents do freely, fully and absolutely give, grant, bargain, sell, alien, enfeoffe and confirme unto the said John Saffin, his heires, Exec'rs, Adm'rs and assignes forever One share or two and twentyeth part of

Atherton to Saffin

all and singular the Lands lying and being in the Narraganset
Country in New England afore s'd and Countrys adjacent,
which were formerly

(26) mortgage by the Indian Sachems unto my S'd deceased ffather & his Associates, (which Lands are since forfited
and possession thereof given as by the S'd morgage bearing date
the thirteenth day of October 1660, & other Evidences and
writings relating thereunto may and doth appear TOGETHER
with all rights, profits, liberties, privileges hereditam'ts im-
unitys and appurtenances whatso ever to the premisses belonging or in any wise appertaining, TO HAVE AND TO HOLD the
s'd one share or two & twentyeth part of the s'd Lands with
all and singular, the rights, profits, liberties, emulum'ts,
priviledges, hereditam'ts appurtenances belonging to the same
or any part or parcel thereof, And also all Deeds, writings
and evidences, whatsoever touching and concerning the same
unto the s'd John Saffin, his heirs, Exec'rs, Adm'rs and assignes and to his and their own sole and proper use, benefit
and behoofe for ever, AND I tho s'd Jonathan Atherton for
my selfe, my heirs, Exec'rs and Adm'rs do hereby covenant
and grant to and with the s'd John Saffin his Exec'rs and assignes, That at the time of the bargain and sale hereof and
before the Ensealing and delivery of these presents I was
the true, sole and lawfull owner of all the above granted premisses, & stand lawfully seized and possessed of the same in
my own proper right of a good perfect and absolute Estate
of inheritance in fee simple and had in my selfe full power
and lawfull Authority to grant bargain, sell and assure the
same as afores'd, AND shall and will warrant, and for ever
defend the above granted premisses, & every part and parcel
thereof unto the s'd John Saffin, his heires Exec'rs, Adm'rs
and assignes against all, and every person and persons whatsoever haveing, claiming, or pretending to have or claim any
legall right, title, or interest of, in or to the same by any waise
or meanes whatsoever, AND that I S'd Jonathan Atherton shall

and will at all times hereafter, (upon request made unto me
for that end) doe and performe all such further act or acts,
thing or things, whither by acknowledging this present Deed,
or by giving such farther and ample assurance of all the afore
bargained premisses for the farther confirmation, thereof unto
the S'd John Saffin, his heires Execto'rs, Adm'rs & assign s
as in law or equity can be desired or required IN WITNESS
whereof I the s'd Jonathan Atherton have hereunto set my
hand and seale this first day of May, In the twenty-ninth
yeare of the Reign of S'd Sovereign Lord, Charles the second.
Anno qu Dom 1677   Jonathan Atherton

Locus Sigilli

Signed, Sealed and Deliv'd in the presence of us, Tho. Kelland, Humphry Warren, John Hayward, S'n.

Jonathan Atherton did this day appeare before me and did
acknowledge this deed & Instrum't of Convayance according
to Law. May ye third day, Anno 1677.

Edward Tyng, Asist.
No. 30 Exam.

Boston, May 24th 1684.

(27) By the Com itte Appointed & Impowered to manage
& order the affaires Respecting the Mortgaged Lands in the
Naraganset Country.

Whereas at several meetings at Boston of sundry of the
Propiet'rs of the Lands of Naraganset caled the Mortgage
Lands upon the 11th Octo'r Last and sundry other times
Computation haveing been made of the Charge, Expence &
debts of Late years, Contracted for defence of sd Interest &
what is for ther Necessary to obtaine his Maj'ties, Confirmation of Propriety and whereas sundry Consultations have been
had to finde ways or meanes by wch mony may be most
Equally Advanced, and Considering that the several p'sons
whose names were Entered as partners with Maj'r Atherton in

S'd Lands were only admitted upon Condition that they beare a proportion of all Charge in that Concerne, many of whom have been hither too at no charge or disburse about it. And, whereas, sundry proposals have been made & Indeavors used to borrow or Raise money to defray the afore s'd orders, and charge upon the Credit & Interest of the S'd Lands, but none that have been treated wch have been willing to advance there on, & that hither to the Charge hath Loined upon som few it hath been thought fitt & Needfull, & Resolved that each partner for a single share, & shall & ought to Contribute twenty pounds in Money, & pay the same to Capt. Elisha Hutchinson, in Boston, within too Months after the date hereof, who keeps & will Render accounts how the same shal be disbursed, & that those that shal make default of payment as afore s'd, shal & will be Justly Excluded & shut out from all propriety & Interest therein & looked upon as unconcerned in S'd Lands, of wch all persons Admitted upon the Conditions afores'd are hereby desired to take notis & accordingly act, applaying themselves to the standing Com itte to be Resolved in any thing doubtful in & about the p'mises.

No. 31 Exam.

By order of the President & Council:

Wee, John Pinchon, Bartholomew Gedney & Jonathan Tyng, Members of his Majties Councill, have Examined the several acts, accords, Deeds and Entrys in the twenty seven foregoing pages, & finde them to agree with the Originals in the hands of Capt. Elisha Hutchinson, And Recomend it to the President & Council, that the transactions in this booke be allowed and declared good and Authentick Records, and that the same Booke be Caryed on & Imployed for Entry of the subsequant acts, orders, agreements and transactions of the proprietors deriveing by, with & from Jno. Winthrop, Esq., and Maj'r Hump'ry Atherton, deceased, & there Associates, and all other Matters fitt for publique Record in the Naraganset Country, or King's Providence.

Boston, the 17th day of June,   John Pynchon,
1686.   Barth'l Gedney.
allowed by ye President,   Jonathan Tyng.
& Councill. Ed. Randolph, Sec'y.

(28) Rochester, in the King's Providence, June 23th, 1686.

At a general Meeting of the Proprietors of the mortgage lands.

Whereas, at severall meetings of the said propriet'rs Certaine gent men and others have bin admited joynt part'rs in the said mortgaged lands with the proprietors, But noe deed nor Coveynant as yett past unto them from the proprit'rs for their Respective interests.

It is ordered and agreed by the propriet'rs and Com ittee then present that Richard Wharton, Elisha Hutchinson and John Saffin, Esqrs., be and are hereby apointed a Com ittee in the name and behalfe of the whole Company to signe and seale deeds for such Respective parts and interests which shall be good and valued in law to all intents and purposes as if it signed by the whole number of proprietors; further, it is agreed that any one member of the S'd Com ittee, or Maj'r Richard Smith, Capt. John Browne or Capt. Natheniel Thomas are hereby appointed and Impowered in the name of the s'd Company of propriet'rs to Commence and presecute and to hold plea & defend any Reall action Reffering to any part or parcell of the said Mortgage lands, or damage against any intruders or Ileagall posses'srs whatsoever, according to law, and untill further ord'rs from the Propriet'rs or Comittee a fore s'd.

Richard Wharton Esq.
Elisha Hutchinson Esq.
and John Saffin Esq.
appointed Comittee

Rochester, Jan'y 24th, 1686.

The aforegoing ord'rs by the Court and agreem't being presented to ye Court and their allowance thereon prayed, It is ordered and declared that ye same bee allowed and is Rattified, and that the Clerke of the Courte and Record'r of the premisses doe each of them Record the Same.

Enter'd upon Record this 28th June, 1686, p'r

Jno. Fones, Record'r.

(29) James, the second, by the grace of God, King of England, Scotland, france and Ireland, Defender of the faith, &c. To all to whome these pres'ts shall come, greete-

Kings Commis-
sion to
President &
Council

ing: WHEREAS, a writte of Scire Facias hath bin Issued out of ye high court of Chancery ag'nst the late Gover'r and Company of the Massachusetts Bay, in New England, whereby ye Governm't of that Collony and members thereof is now in s'd hands, and wee being minded to give all Prottection and incourigem't to s'd good Subjects therein, and to provide in the most Effectuall man'r that due and impartiall justice maye bee administered in all Cases, civill & criminall, and that all possible care maye be taken for the just, quiett and orderly Governm't of the same. Know yee, therefore, that wee, by and wth ye advice of o'r privy Councill, have thought fitt to Errect and constitute, and by these presents for us o'r heirs and Suceso'rs, do Errect, constitute and apoint a President and Councill to take care of all that o'r territory and Dominion of New England, In America, com'noly called and Known by the name of or Collony of the Massachusetts Bay, and o'r Province of New hampshire and maine and the Narragansett Country, otherwise called ye Kings Province, wth all the Islands rights and members there unto appurtaineing and to ord'rly rule, and Governe ye same according to such method of and Regulations as are herein after Specyified and Declared untill o'r chiefe Gov'r shall arrive within o'r S'd Collonys, and for ye bett'r Execution of o'r Royall pleasure, in this behalfe wee doe hereby nominate and appointe o'r trusty and well beloved subject, Joseph Dudley, Esq., to bee ye first Presid't of the said Council, and to continue in the said office untill wee o'r heires or Successo'rs shall otherwise direct, and wee doe like wise nominate and appointe o'r trusty and well belloved Subjects, Simon Bradstreete, Wm. Stoughton, Pett'r Bulkley, John pynchon, Rob't Mason, R. Wharton, Waite Winthrop, Nath'l Saltonstall, Bartholomew Gedney, Jonathan Tyng, John Usher, Dudley Bradstreete, John

Hinkes, Francis Champernoone, Edward Tyng, Jno. Fitz Winthrop and Edward Randolph Erqs. to bee of o'r Councill within o'r said territory and Collony and, and that ye s'd Jos. Dudley & every succeeding president of the said Councill shall and maye nominate and appointe any one of ye members of the said councill for the time being to be his deputy and to Preside in his absence, and that the said Presid't or his Depuety, and any Seven of the Said councill shall bee a Quorum and o'r Express will and pleasure is that no person shall bee admitted to sitt or have a vote in ye said councill until hee have taken ye oath of aleigeance and the oath hereafter mentioned for the due and impartiall Execution of Justice, and the faithfull Discharge of ye trust in th'm Reposed which oathes wee doe hereby authorize and derrict the s'd Simon Bradstreete, Wm. Stoughton, Petter Bulkley, John Pynchon, Rob Mason, Rich Wharton, Waite Winthrop, Nathaniel Saltonstall, Bartholomew Gedney, Jonathan Tyng, John Usher, Dudley Bradstreete, John Hinkes, Fra. Champernoone,

(30) Edward Tyng, John Fitz Winthrop and Edw. Randolph or any three of them, first to administer unto ye said Jos. Dudley the first President and ye said Joseph Dudley haveing taken ye said oathes wee doe, will authorize and require him and the presid't for the time being to administer the same from tyme to time to all and Every other the members of o'r s'd Council, and wee doe here by will and require and command o'r S'd Presid't and Council and every of them to whom this o'r pleasure Shall bee made Knowne, yt all Excesses whatsoever Sett apart they faile not to assemble and meet together at o'r towne of Boston, in New England, as Soon as may bee within the space of twenty dayes at the farthest next after ye arrivall of this our Commission at o'r said towne of Boston, and when to cause our commission or letters Pattent to bee read before such of them as shall be there assembled to gether to the Examplisation of the Ingag-

m't passed in o'r high court of Chancery against the said
late Govern'r and Company of the Massachusetts Bay, and
haveing duly first taken the said oathes together to choose,
nominate and appoint such Officers and Servants as they shall
think fitt and nessesairey for o'r Service, and alsoe to appoint
Such other time and place for their future meetings as they
or the Maj'r part of them, whereof the presid't o'r his
Deputy to be One Shall think fitt and agree, and our will
and pleasure is yt our said Councill shall from time to time
have and use such Seale, Onley for ye Sealeing their acts &
orders & proceeding as shall bee appointed by us o'r heirs and
Success'rs for that purpose, and we doe by these presents, o'r
heires and Succeso'rs Constitute, Establish, declare and appoint o'r said Presid't and Councill & their Successo'rs for
the time being to bee a compleat and settled court of Record
for the administration of Justice to all o'r Subjects inhabiting within the limits aforesaid in all cases as well Civill as
criminall, and yt the Presid't or any Seven of the Councill
for the time being shall have full pow'r and authoritie to
hold plea in all cases from time to time, as well as pleas of
ye Crowne, and in all matters Rellating to ye Condemation
of the peace and punishm't of Offenders, as in civill Suites
and actions betweene P'ty and party, or between us or any of
o'r Subjects there, whether ye Same doe concerne ye Really
and Relate to any right or freehold and inheritance, and
whether ye Same doe Concerne ye personally, and relate to
Some matters of debt contract, Damage or other personall
injury, and alsoe in all mixt actions which may concerne both
realty ann Personalty, and therein after due, and Orderly
proceeding and Deliberate heareing on both sides to give
Judgement and to award Execution as well in criminall as
Civill cases, as afores'd, see allways yt the formes of proceedings in Such cases, and the Judgm'ts thereupon to be given be
as consonant and agreeable to the Laws and Statutes of this
o'r Realme of England, as the present State and condition
of o'r Subjects Inhabiting within the limits aforesaid, and

the Circumstances of the place will admitt, and the presid't &

(**31**) and Councill for ye time being, and every one of them Respectively before they bee admitted to there Severall and Respective offices and charges Shall alsoe take ye oath— oath followinge ———— you shall Swear well and truly to administer Justice to all his Maj'ties good Subjects inhabiting within ye territory and Dominion of New England, und'r this his Maj'ties Government, and also duely, faithfully to discharge and Execute the trust in you reposed, accordinge to ye best of yo'r knowledge, you shall Spare no person for favours or affection, nor any p'son grieve for hattred or Ill will, So help you God, and wee doe further hereby give and grant unto o'r said President and Councill, or to ye Maj'r part of them, full pow'r and authoritie to Errect, Constitute and establish Such and soe many County Courts and other Inferior Courts of Judicature and publicke Justice within o'r said Colony and Dominion as they shall think fitt and necessary for the hearing and Determining of all causes as well causes as well criminall as civill according to law and equitie, and for awarding of Execution there upon with all reasonable and nessessary powers, authorities, fees and privilidges, Bellongeing unto them. Nevertheless it is our will and pleasure, and Soe wee doe hereby Expressely Declare that it shall and maye be lawfull from time to time to send for all & every p'son who shall think him or them selves agrieved by any Sentence, Judgement or Decree, pronounced, given or made as aforesaid in, aboute or concerning ye title of any land or other reall Estate or any p'sonall Action or Suite above ye value of three hundred pounds, & not und'r to appeale from Such Judgem't & Sentence or Decree unto us in o'r privy Councill, but wch and und'r This caution and Limittation yt the appealeant Shall first Enter wch and give good Securitie to pay full costs in case noe estate shall bee Claimed upon Such appeale, and for the better Defence and Securitie of all o'r loveing Subjects within o'r said territory and Dominion of New England Our further will and pleasure is and wee doe hereby authoritize, Require and command o'r said presid't and Councill for the time being in o'r name and und'r ye Seale by us appointed or to bee appointed, to be used to give and Issue forth commissions from time to time to such person and persons whom they shall Judge best quaalified for the Regulations and Discipline of the Militia of our said territory and Dominion, and for the arraying and mustering the inhabitants thereof, and instructing them how to beare and use their armes, and that care be taken that Such good Discipline shall be observed as by the said Council shall be prescribed, and yt if any invasions shall at any time bee made, or other destruction, Detriment or annoyance made or done by indians or others upon or unto o'r good Subjects inhabiting within ye said territory and Dominion, wee, by these presents, for us, our heires and successo'rs, Declare, ordaine and grant that it shall and maye be lawfull to and for our said Subjects So commissioned by o'r said councill from time to time, and at all times, for their Special Defence and Saftie to Encounter, Expel, Repeal and resist by force of armes and

(32) all other fitting wayes, and means whatsoever all and every Such p'son and p'sons as shall at any time hereafter attempt or Enterprise the distruction, invasion, detriment or annoyance of any our Said loveing Inhabitants or their plantations or Estates, and above all thinges wee doe by these presents will require and Command o'r said councill to take all possible care for the discounteniancing of all vice and incourigem't of virtue and good liveing, that by such Example, the infidells mayebe invited and desier to, P'take of the Christian Relligion and for the greater Ease & Sattesfaction of our said loveing Subjects in matters of Relligion, wee doe hereby will, require and command yt libertie of consciouce

shall bee alowed unto all P'sons, and yt such Espectialy as shal bee conformable to ye rights of the church of England, shall bee particularly conutenanced and incouraged.

and further, wee doe by these presents for us, o'r heires and Successo'rs, give and grant unto ye Sayd Council and their Successo'rs, for the time being full and free liberty, power and authority, to hear & determine in all Emergances, Rellateing to ye peace and good Governm't of our Subjects, within ye s'd province and also to Sumon and Convene, any p'son or p'sons before y'm and punish Contempt's and to cause the oath of aleigiance to bee administered to all and every p'son and p'sons who shall bee admitted to any office or preferment and for Supporting the charge of o'r government of o'r said territory and Dominion In New England. Our will and pleasure is and wee doe by these presents authorize, and Require the said Presid't and Councill to continue Such taxes and Impositions as have bin and are now laid and imposed upon the inhabitants thereof, and that they levey and Distribute or cause the same to be leveyed and Distributed to these ends, in the best and most equall manner they can alsoe, our will and pleasure is and wee doe hereby derrect and appoint, that if the s'd Presid't of our Councill shall happen to dye, that then from and after the death of the s'd president, his deputy shal Succeed him in the office of president, and, Shall and maye nominate and chose any one of ye Said council to be his deputy to preside in his absence, and the said Deputy Succeeding Shall continue in the said Office of president untill o'r further will and pleasure be Knowne therein, and if any of ye members of the s'd council shall hapen to dye, our will and pleasure is and wee doe hereby dirrect and appoint the presid't of o'r Council for the time being to Elect Some other person to bee a member of the said Council for that time, and to send over ye name of such p'son soe chosen, and the names of two more whom o'r president Shall judge fittly qualified for the s'd trust, that wee our heires and successo'rs maye nominate and appointe which of the three Shall bee ye member in the place of ye member Soe dyeing and Lastly o'r will and pleasure is that The said president and Councill for the tyme being do prepare

(**33**) and send unto us Such Rules and methords for their owne proceedings as maye best Suite with ye Constitution of o'r territory and Dominion aforesd, and for the best Establishing our Authoritie there, and the Government thereof, that wee maye alter or approve the Same as wee shall think fitt;
In Witness whereof wee have caused these o'r Lett'rs to be made Pattent.
Witness o'r selfe at Westminister, the 8th day of Octo., in the first yeare of o'r Raigene.

Ea. Randolph, Sec'y.

A true Copie.

By the Presid't and Councill of his Maj'ties territory and Dominion of New England in America.

To Joseph Dudley, William Stoughton, John Winthrop, Edward Randolph and Rich Wharton, John Blackwell, Edward Palmer and Samuell Sewall Esqs, Elisha Hutchinson, Richard Smith, Francis Brinley, Jno. Saffin Esqs., John Fones, Thomas Ward & James Pendleton, Gent &c.

Joseph Dudley Presid't.

Know ye yt wee his maj'ties Presid't and Councill by virtue *Councils Commission to ye Justices.* of authoritie, to us given by this, his Maj'ties Commission und'r ye greate Seale of England for Governm't of this his Maj'ties said Territory and Dominion, bearing date at Westminster, ye Eight day of Octo'r. In the first yeare of his Reigne, have nominated, appointed and assigned you, and every such or more of you whereof, the said Joseph Dudley or Wm. Stoughton or John Winthrop, Is to be one of his

Maj'ties Justice of ye peace and Commission'rs within ye Narragansett Country, otherwise, called ye Kings province to settle and dispose the affaires of yt Province, and ye people thereof accordinge to such methods and Regulations as are hereafter Specified and declared untill wee shall otherwise order and wee doe hereby will and require you his Maj'ties Said Justices and Commissioners and every of you yt all Excesses whatsoever, Sett apart you faile not to assemble and meet togethes at Maj'r Richard Smiths, in the Narragansett Country and hold a Courte in his Maj'ties name at or upon Wensdaye ye 23 th Daye of this instant June, and then and there to cause his Maj'ties Commission or Letters, Pattent or ye Exemplification or Copie thereof attested by the Secretary of his Maj'cies Councill here and this his Maj'ties Commission for constituting this Court to bee publickly read and to appoint Such officers and servants and Such other time and place for yo'r future meetings, as you or any three or more of you whereof you ye Said Joseph Dudley or Wm. Stoughton or John Winthrop to be one, Shall think fitt and agree on for his Maj'ties service, and yt you the Said Joseph Dudley, Wm. Stoughton, John Winthrop, Edward Randolph, Richard Wharton, or any of you or any other member of his Maj'ties Councill together with any two of ye Justices of ye peace hereafter named, and in absence of all and every member of his Maj'ties Councill you the said John Blackwell, Edward Palmer, Samuel Seawall, Elisha Hutchinson, Rich Smith, Francis Brinley and John Saffin, who are by this Commission, all assigned to be Justices of ye peace and of ye Quorum or any one of you together with any two others of ye Justices of ye peace Viz.: John ffones, Thomas Ward and James Pendleton shall have power, and are hereby authorized and appointed to be a constant and Settled Court, for ye Administration of Justice to all his Maj'ties, Subjects inhabiting within ye Limitts of his majesties,

(**34**) said province and all ye rights and members thereunto appurtaineing in all Cases as well Civill as criminall, and shall have full pow'r and Authority to hold plea in all Cases, from time to time as well, in pleas of ye Crowne and in all matters rellating to ye Consideration of ye peace and punishment of Offenders, not Extending to Life or Limb, as in all Civill Suites or actions, Betweene p'tye and pa'rties or betweene his Maj'ties and any of his Maj'ties Subject, whether the Same doe concerne the Personalty and relate to some maner of deed and contract Damage, and other personall injurey and alsoe in all mixt actions wch maye concerne both Realty and personalty, and therein after due and orderly proceeding and Deliberate heareing of both Sides to give Judgment and to award Execution, not Extending to life or Limb as aforesaid as well in criminall as in Civill Cases as aforesaid, See alsoe yt ye formes of proceedings in Such cases and ye Judgm't there upon to be Given, be as Consonant, and agreeable to ye Laws and Statutes of his Maj'ties Realme of England, as the present State and Condition of his Maj'ties Subjects inhabiting within ye limitts aforesaid, and Circumstances of the place will admitt, haveing always due regard to his Maj'ties, Gracious indulgence for Libertie of conscience in matter of Relligion, and in case any person Shall be charged before you with any Capittall Offence or crime against his Maj'tie, his Governm't or authoritie, then you are to committ him to safe custodie & upon any probable Evidence of his Guilt, and Recognizance taken for prosecution, you are to send Such person under safe guard and custody, to bee delivered up to ye ord'r of ye Presid't, or other of his Maj'ties Councill at Boston, and you and every one of you respectively before you be admitted to ye Exercise of ye power afores'd, shall take this Oath following ——— you shall swear well and truely to administer Justice to all his Maj'ties good Subjects inhabiting within the territory and Dominion of New England und'r this his Maj'ties Government, and alsoe duely and faithfully to discharge and Execute ye trust in you reposed, according to ye best of yo'r Knowledge, you shall Spare noe person for fevour of affection nor any person Grieve for hattred or Ill will, So help you God ═══════ which said oath wee doe hereby authorize you the s'd Joseph Dudley, Wm. Stoughton, John Winthrop, or any other member of his Maj'ties Councill or Justice of ye Quorum to Administer, nevertheless wee his Maj'ties, Presid't and Councill doe hereby Expressly Declare yt shall and maye be lawfull from time to time, To and for all and every person yt that shall Think him or themselves agrieved by any sentenced Judgment or Decree pronounced, Given or made as aforesaid, In aboute or concerneinge ye, The title of Land or other reall Estate or in any personall action or Suite above ye value of tenn pounds and not und'r to appeale from such Judgement, Sentence or Decree unto us his Maj'ties, Said Presid't and Councill, But wch and und'r this Caution and Limmittation, yt the appealant Shall first enter unto and give good Secuereitie to paye full costs in Case, in Reliefe Shall be Obtained upon such appeale and for the better Deffence and Securety of his Maj'ties Loveing Subjects within the said province, wee his Maj'ties, Presid't and Councill aforesaid doe hereby authorize you or any three or more of you, whereof he said Joseph Dudley, Wm. Stoughton or Jno. Winthrop or some other member of the councill or In their absence, you, John Blackewell, Edward Palmer, Samuell Seawall, Elisha Hutchinson, Rich'd Smith to be one of his Maj'ties Com'ss'rs for ye Ordering Reguleation, and Discipline of ye Militia of his

(35) said Province for ye arrayeing and mustering the inhabitants thereof, and instructing them how to beare and use their arms, and to take care of such good Discipline rules and orders be Observed as by his Maj'ties, Said Presid't and Councill Shall be prescribed and from time to time to nominate unto us his Maj'ties, said presid't and Councill, the names of such persons upon or within ye Said province as you Shall Judge fitt to be appoint-

ed Commanders and other Officers of the said Militia, and to administer to all Such commanders and Military Offercers, and to all Justices of the peace, constables and other Offercers allready appointed and Commissioned in all or any the affairs of his Maj'ties in the said province that have not alreadye in due forme, taken ye same as well the Oath of Allegiance appointed by Law, as the Oath herein before reciated for ye faithfull and due Discharge of their respective offices trusts and Imploym'ts and above all things wee his Maj'ties, Said Presid't and Councill doe by these presents will and require you and every of you his Maj'ties Commissioners In the affaires hereby Committed to you to take all possible care for ye Discountenanceing all vice and incouragem't of v'rtue and good Liveing, that by such Example ye Infidells maye be Invited and Desire to partake of the Christian Religion.

And wee doe further hereby give and Grant to you or any three or more of you, whereof ye S'd Joseph Dudley, Wm. Stoughton or John Winthrop or some member of his Maj'ties Councill, or in their absence, you, the said John Blackwell, Edward palmer, Elisha Hutchinson, Rich'd Smith, fra. Brinley or John Saffin to be one full and free liberties, power and authority to heare and Determine in all Emergenciees rellating to ye power and good Governm't of his Maj'ties Subjects within the Said Kings Provinces, and alsoe to summon and Convene any person or persons before you to punish Contempts and to cause pe oath of alegiance to be administered to all and every person and persons who shall be admitted into any office or Preferment within the Same Province in Witness whereof wee have caused this o'r Commission to be attached and Ratified under ye Seale appointed by his Maj'tie for Confirmation of the publick Acts and ord'rs and Commissions of us his Maj'ties, Said Councill, Dated at Boston, the 18th day of June, In the second yeare of his Maj'ties reigine.   By order of the Presid't and Councill,

Edward Randolph, Secre'ty.

(36)   To the Kings most Excellent Maj'ty

Maye it Please yo'r Majesty,

Whereas yo'r Maj'tie hath bin graceously Pleased by yo'r Commission und'r yo'r Royall Signett, beareing date att Whitehall ye seventh day of aprill in the four and thirtieth yeare of yo'r Reigine to Constitute Edward Cranfield Esq'r, Lieuten't Gov'r and Command'r in Chiefe of new Hampshire, William Stoughton, Joseph Dudley, Edward Randolph, Samuel Shrimpton, John Fitz Winthrop, Edward Palmer, John Pynchon and Nathaniel Saltinstall Esq'rs or any three of them whereof Edward Cranfield or Edward Randolph Should bee of ye Corum Com'rs for Enquireing into the Respective Claimes, and titles as well of yo'r Maj'ties as all p'sons and Corporations whatsoever to ye imediate Jurrisdiction and Propriety of Soyle to the Kings Province or Narragansett Countriy and to make Reporte of ye Same, wth theire Oppinions upon ye matter yt Should bee Examined by them, That yo'r Maj'tie might cause impartiall Justice to bee done

In Humble Obedience to yo'r Maj'ties Command, wee yo'r Maj'ties Sayd Commissioners whose names are Subscribed doe humbley offer yt upon receipt of yo'r Said Commission wee both by yo'r Lett'rs to yo'r Severall Govern'rs and councill, of yo'r Collonies and by printed Summons Sent to them to Publish if they Saw cause in their Respective Jurrisdiction for information of their people, Signified ye purport of ye Said Commission, and yt wee had appointed on Wens daye the two and twentieth of Aug't, to Convene at ye house of mr. Rich'd Smith in ye Narragansett Countrey to receive all such information, Evidence and claime as well in yo'r Maj'ties behalfe as of all p'sons and Corporations whatsoever as should bee offered wth other Nessessary Instructions & that upon the two and twentieth of Aug'st, wee convened at ye place aforesaid where Capt. John Allyn and mr. John Wadsworth two of the Majestrates of Conecticott Collony as their agentes, Thomas Hinckley Esq'r Gov'r of New Plymouth In person and mr Waite Winthrop, mr. Symon Lynde, mr. John Saffin, mr.

Elisha Hutchinson, mr. Richard Wharton and mr. Joshiah Lambe in thire owne Behalfe and as Representatives for ye Rest that claime Propriety in Right of John Winthrop Esq'r and Majo'r Humphrey Atherton and Parteners, all Appeared and after every duty full and thankfull acknowledgm'ts of yo'r Maj'ties great and gracious care to informe yo'r Selfe and by yo'r final Determination to cause impartiall Justice to bee done. The Agents of Conecticott and Gov'r of New Plymouth in theire Collonies Behalfe Respectively claimed Jurrisdiction by pattent over the Kings Province or Narragansett countrey, and the said mr. Winthrop, Lynde, Saffin, Hutchinson, Wharton and Lambe, Entered their claimes and produced their Evidences for the Soyle of the said Province and countrey. Sundry Other Claimes were alsoe Exhibited to Severall parts of ye Said Province, all P'sons any waise concerned Expressing grate Sattisfaction in and Submittion to yo'r Maj'ties Commands and our proceedings, Excepte Onley ye Governm't of Rhoad Island aud Providence Plantations, from whom accordinge to the Informations given to yo'r Maj'ties Commissionr'es

(37) Anno, 1664, and what was Some yeares Since Suggested to yo'r Maj'tie and Councill by Randall Houldeen and John Greene, wee Expected further Information as Evidence as to yo'r Maj'tys interest and Propriety, but in steed of their Collonies Assistance in yo'r Maj'ties Concernes and prosecution of their owne prettension, their Genereall Assembly was promptly called and as wee are informed adjourned in an unusuall manner to a house in the Narragansett Countrey, distant about a mile from ye place of our Session who Sent us a Lett'r interdicting o'r Proceedings which not availeing thye Sent their Sergeant Generall in a Riotus mann'r wth a greate number of horsemen who by Loud Proclamation Prohibited us from Keepeing court in any Part of their Jurrisdiction, Commanding all persons within ye Verge of their Collonie or Kings Province to Depart and not to bee abett'rs to our pre-

tended Court, as by their Lett'r & Proclamation Maye more fully Appeare Nothwithstanding wee continued to make Stricte Enquirey and Examination both of the Ancientest Inhabitants of ye English and Indians for two dayes and received all such claimes as were presented & in Regard nowe Appeared wth any claime or plea in yo'r Maj'ties behalfe, wee Adjourned to Boston there to meet on the third of September following, and Substituted a Committee to carry a Lett'r to Rhoad Island court intimeteing our Adjournm't and Demand in yo'r Maj'ties name and for yo'r behalfe, yt ye said Committee might Striete Judge and Examine their Records, and alsoe sent particular sumons in yo'r Maj'ties name to said Houldin and Greene to appeare before us on the third of September, and to give in Evidence pursuant to ye Information or Suggestion given to yo'r Maj'ty in Councill at Whitehall, which said Lett'r was delivered to mr. William Coddington their Governor, and ye Sumons to ye Said John Greene, in Open Court, the Answer and Responce wherof and the methods of our Proceedings and of ye greate contempt Offered to your Maj'ties Commission by ye Gen'll Assembly of Rhoad Island, wee humbly Reffer To a Narrative drawne by William Wharton our Reg'r and approved by our Selves which with this will by our Ord'rs bee humbly laid at yo'r Maj'ties feete.

Upon Monday the third of S'd September wee againe convened at Boston and gave further Opportunities for New Claimes, but none from Rhoad Island Appeared, Soe yt they then faileing In their duty, mr. Richard Wharton and partners Exhibited a printed booke containgeinge a Deed beareing Date the 19th of aprill 1644, being the Subjection of two chiefe Sachems named, Pissicuss and Canonicus of themselves, their people and lands to the care, Protection and Governm't of yo'r Royall father of blessed memory and wth the Said Booke was presented a Breviate or memoriall of ye Occaission and Improvement of Said Subjection, the said Wharton and parten'rs Declaireinge that none of them Know of any other Evidence as to yo'r Maj'ties Propriety or interest in ye Soyle, nither hath any bin Offered by any other hand, Soe That wee have Primirly and Seriously considered ye Severall claimes Before us to ye Jerrisdiction which wee finde as well by the Said printed Deed of Subjection as by former Capitulations and conclussions after Conquest of the Pequods Betweene ye Maj'ties Subjects of the United Collonies and the Sachems (38) and Consello'rs in the Narragansett Countrey and the Purchase, Possession and Improvement made by yo'r Maj'ties Subjects to have bin Absolutely vested in yo'r Maj'ty and yt yo'r Maj'ty by yo'r Letters Pattents dated at Westminster the three and twentieth of April, in the fourteenth yeare of yo'r Maj'ties Reigne yo'r Maj'ty granted to ye Gov'r and Company of Connecticott and their Success'ors all that part of yo'r Dominion in New England, Bounded on the East by Narragansett River, comonlly called Narragansett Bay, Where the said River falleth into ye Sea, and on the North by the Line of ye Massachusetts Plantation, and on the South by the Sea and in Longitude as ye Lyne of the Massachusetts Running from East to West that is to Saye from ye Said Narragansett Bay on the East to the South Sea on the west part, there unto adjourneing together with all firme lands, Soyles, grounds, Havens, Ports, Pointes, Watters, fishings, Mines, miniralls, precious stones, and all and Singular other Commodities and Jurrisdictions whatsoever Reserving to yo'r Maj'ty, yo'r heires and Successors, Only the fifth part of ye Oare of Gold and Silver as by the said Charte maye at Large appeare.

Wee have alsoe had Information, yt Sometime after yo'r Maj'tys grant and Said Pattent was Sent to yo'r Collonies of Connecticott, the said Countrey of the Narragansett was Likewise by Pattent granted by yo'r Ma'ty to ye Gov'r & Compa. of Rhoad Island Plantation, and is by Charter bounded by a River called Pawquatuck which by said Charter is for ever to bee accounted and called the Narragansett River, and this Latter grant of yo'r Maj'ty to Rhoad Island Seemes to bee founded upon advice Submitted to, by John Winthrop esquire, Sayd to bee Agent for Connecticott Collony and mr. John Clarke Agent for Rhoad Island to which the Agents of Connecticutt plead that mr. Winthrops Agency for them wase when hee had Obtained and Sent ye Pattent to them, & that noe Submission or act of his could Invalidate or deprive them of any the benefitts graciously granted by yo'r Maj'tys Charter and yt Notwithstandeing the Seemeinge Bounderries, Sett by the said Articles Signed by mr. Winthrop and mr. Clarke, Itt is in ye same Articles provided yt the Propriet'rs and Inhabittants of the Narragansett Countrey, Shall chuse to which of the two Governments to belong, and yt they unanimously chose and Subjected to the Government of Connecticott und'r which yt Plantation began to prosper till ye yeare 1664-5 when Some of yo'r Maj'ties Commissionrs (which it is alledged without Collonell Nicholls,) then absent, (could make noe valid act) In favour to ye Rhoad Islanders, Published some Inadvertent Ord'rs Sent by Collonell Nicholls and themselves Reversed however by the said Ord'rs and the prettensions that the Rhoad Islanders by virtue of their Pattent make Wee finde they have much Mollested the Inhabitants and Discouraged the Settlement of the said Countrie and occassioned Continuall Controversies betweene the said Collonies.

Pursuant therefore to yo'r graciouis Ends to quiett these Disputes, wee have Carefully Endeavoured to Obleague certaine Knowledge of the boundes of yo'r Maj'ties Councill of the Narragansett Countriey and upon ye best Evidence offered and Examination of Sundry Ancient persons both of the English and Indians, It appears yt a Brooke called Wecapaug is neare the Sea the westerly bounds of the Narragansett Country, all the land

(39) which is in bredth aboute fouer or five miles, Lyeing betweene the said Brooke and Pauquatuck being the Pequod Conntrey, and by Conquest taken from them and dispossed of to Severall p'sons within which Limitts

Lyes Said farmes bellongeing by Ancient grant, to Harvard Colledge, to mr. Symon Lynde & other persons whose titles being asserted have bin Acknowledged by all others Pretending Propriety, and yt the Narragansett Bay or River where it fall into ye Sea bounds ye Narragansett Countrey Easterly and by a testymoney given by Gov'r Winthrop in his Life time upon another occassion, and alsoe by Information of Sundry Old and principall Indians, It appeares that Patuckett River lyeing betweene Rehoboth and Providence was ye intended boundery, and lines betweene Plimouth Collonie and Providence plantation which in Plimouth Pattent is called Narragansett River, the Patucket river fallinge into the greater Narragansett River or Bay that bounds Narragansett, Eastward Soe, yt betweene ye Said River of Patuckett Quenebaug and Nipmug countries to ye Northward and Wecapaug Brooke, Westerly Lyes the whole Dominion and territory containing the Cowhesett and Niantick Countreys, formerly and lately bellonging to ye Narragansett Sachems and generally called the Narragansett Countrey as doth claime made by the Colloney of Plimouth to Jurrisdiction and Toycheing Narragansett Countrey, wee finde it hath onley foundation from ye name given to Pawquatuck of ye Narragansett River, (and if Anciently and truely soe called then Plimouth's charter if confirmed by yo'r Maj'ty being granted by the Councill of Plimouth and beares date the 13th of January, In the fifth yeare of ye Reigine of yo'r Royall father) will Determine ye Controversee Betweene Rhoad Island and Connecticott, and Comprehends ye whole Narragansett and part of the Pequod Countrey, the Lands granted to plimouth, being bounded Southerly by the Narragansett River, But with humble Submission wee cannot See any cause to Judge yt the said Pawquatuck Riv'r Anciently was o ought to bee called or accounted ye Narragansett River, Because it Lyes Some miles within the Pequod Countrey a Nation till Exterpated by the English often or allwaise at warr wth ye Narragansetts, and to which Territorys ye Nar-

ragansetts never planted, because Pawquatuck River falls
into ye Sea many miles to ye westward of any part of Narragansett Bay, Wee are of Opinion that ye Narragansett Bay
is the River Anciently called Narragansett River, both because
it on the Eastward washes and boundes ye whole length of
the Narragansett Countrey and for that, Plimouth Colloney
which hath now bin planted neare three score yeares have
ever since bounded themselves accordeinge to ye tearme and
Limittation of their Pattent, by the Same Bay called Narragansett River, towards the South into which ye freshes of
sayd Riv'r called Pacatuck Empties it Selfe in a Precipice,
thus in all hummillitie haveing Represented our opinion as to
the bounds & Jurrisdiction, wee humbly Exprest Our Oppinions Respecting Proprietie of Soyle as followeth:

Wee finde that by one Deed Dated ye Eleventh of June
1659, Coginaquand chiefe Sachem and Proprieto'r of the
Narragansett Countrie did give, grant and conveye to John
Winthrop Esq'r and Maj'r Humphrey Atherton and Partners,
their heires and assignes one lardge tract

(40) of land now called
ye Northward tract, and ye sayd Coginaquand by another
deede dated ye 4th of July 1659, did in like manner conveye
to ye said John Winthrop, Maj'r Atherton and Parten'rs,
another lardge Peace of land now called ye Southerne tracte
or Namecock and wee finde by Sundrye other Deeds from ye
Other Sachems, the sayd Conviances Ratified and Sundry
Receipts and acknowledgm'ts of full Sattisfaction to all p'sons
any waies concerned.

Wee alsoe finde that by a deed beareing date the 13th of
Octo. 1660, Sequenck, Ninaguatt, Scuttup and Quequaganuett, Narragansett Sachems for valuable consideration
Mortgaged to Maj'r Atherton and Parten'rs, the remaineing
parte of ye whole Narragansett Countrey containeing the
Cowhesett and Niantick Countreys, and find yt as part of yt
Consideration Seven hundred thirty four fathom of Peague

was payd Novemb'r 16th, 1660, and Sundry other pyaments made and gratuities given to full Sattisfaction as by Sundry receipts and acknowledgm'ts doth appeare, (the Commisso'rs of all yo'r Maj'ties Collonies approveing these transactions and alsoe Wee finde by the testimonies of John Button, William Cotton, John Rhoades and Ambrose Leech, Sworne before John Endicott Esq'r, Gov'r of the Massachusetts, the 22th of Septemb'r, 1662, and Recorded at Hartford, yt Scuttup and Ninaguatt wth Sundry other Sachems Consello'rs and Indians to the Number of two or three hundred being assembled at a place called Petaquamscott, the said Scuttup in presence of sayd Indians and many English alsoe assembled did in the behalfe of him selfe, brother and friends delliver possession of the Countrey by turff and twigg to Capt. Edward Hutchinson, Capt William Hudson and mr. Richard Smyth, Juno'r, in behalfe of them selves & Partners Declareing the lands to bee then allready Sold by Deede by them selves & the rest of the Saggamores to Maj'r Atherton and Partners.

Wee alsoe finde yt the Said Maj'r Atherton, Capt. Hutchinson, Hudson & partners with grate Expense and Industrey applyed them selves to ye Settlement and Inprovem't of Sayd Countrey, maney Considerable farmes being Layd out, houses and Edifices Errected and two towneship alsoe Layd out, and methods for Improvem'ts and tenures aggreed upon With ye Inhabitants of our townes named, Wickford and ye other Newbury.

Alsoe it Appeares that the said Purchas'rs did Request and Instruct John Winthrop Esq., to Supplicate yo'r Maj'ty to add ye Sayd Narragansett Countrey to the territoryes and Jurrisdiction of Connecticott, which yo'r Maj'ty graciously granted and was further graciously pleased by yo'r Royall Lett'r dated ye 21th of June, 1663, Directed to ye Gover'r and Assistants for the Massachusetts, Plimouth and Connecticott Collonies to Approve and Incourage the Purchasse'rs dessignes and as yo'r Maj'ty pleased them to call them Laudible Evidences to Settle and plant a Colloney to the Enlargem't of yo'r Empire and to Recomende the said Purchasso'rs and Proprieto'rs to the Neighbourly Kindness and Protection of sayd Collonyes willing them upon all Occaissions to bee assisting to them

(41) against the unjust Oppressions and molestations of those of Rhoad Island with other Expressions of yo'r Royall grace and favour to ye Said Purchasers Apon which titles and incouragem'ts the Clayments offer probable Computation and argum'ts that their P'desso'rs them selves and p'sons concerned with them have Expended for purchaseing and Settling the said Countrey at least Twenty thousand Pounds, and that had not ye Ill Effects of the Ord'rs made by some of yo'r Maj'ties Commisso'rs that come Over in 1664, and the greate mollestrations and pretensions of ye Rhoad Islanders Obstructed the Settlement, the Countrey had by ye Planting the Sayd two towns and other Improvem'ts bin Soe Populated that greate part, if not all the mission of the late Indyon warr had bin prevented.

Some other, claimes have bin made by mr. James Noys and others of Some other tract of land lying in ye Niantick Countrey as derieved from Harman Garrett and his son named (———— ————) Pretended Indian Sachem who personally appeared before us, but upon Examination wee cannot finde the said Harman Garrett or his Son had any Righte or pow'r to dispose of any of the Lands, the Same haveing bin Beyonde the memory of man Possessed by Ninigratt, the other Indians acknowledging and testifieing the same.

Other claimes also were Exhibited to Sundry other tracts within the Narragansett Countrey, but the titles being Either derived from or Depending upon mr. Winthrops and Maj'r Athertons Purchases wee humbly conceive more proper for a Court of Judicature.

Thus, after most stricte and Impartiall Inquirey and Examination, haveing Stated wee most humbly laye before yo'r

Maj'ty, the Severall Orriginall claimes and Pretencetions offered to us with Respect to the Propriety both of Jurrisdiction and Soyle in yo'r Maj'ties Province, Or Narragansett Countrey and in furthar Obedience to yo'r s'd Commission have Serriously Weigh'd and considered all Evidences, pleas, promises and Allegations and adee our owne Observations of the course of the Narragansett River or Bay, and Sittuation of the Country Soe farr as wee have travelled therein and with most humble Submission and Reservation of yo'r Maj'ties Right Soe farr as it maye appeare to yo'r Maj'ties Offer, our Oppinion that by vertue of yo'r said Letters, Pattents granted to Connecticott Jurrisdiction in and through the said Province or Narragansett Countrey of Right bellongs to ye Said Colloney of Connecticott, and that propriety of Soyle as Dirrived from mr. Winthrop and Maj'r Atherton is vested in the heires and Assignes of the said mr. Winthrop, the heires of Thomas Cheffinch, Esq'r, Maj'r Atherton, mr. Rich'd Smith, mr. Symon Lynde, mr. Elisha Hutchinson, mr. John Saffin, mr. Richard Wharton and Partners, and Such as dirived from them noe Considerable opposition being by any Corporation or person given before us to their Claime and tittle, the same being granted by the said Agentts

(42) of Connecticott Notwithstanding wee doe not conceive that their Said Purchasses doe any waise Intitle them to any part of the Pequod Countrey lyeinge betweene Wecapauge and Pawquatuck River, nor that ye former lawfull purchasses and possessions of ye Inhabitants of Providence and warwick ought to bee Prejudiced thereby and finally wee hold itt our duty humbly to Informe yo'r Maj'ty that Soe long as the Pretensions of the Rhoad Islanders to ye Governm'ts of Said Provinces continue, itt will much discourage the Settlement & Improvem'ts thereof, it being very Improbable, yt either the afore named Claym'ts or others of like Reputation, and Condition will Either Remove their families or Expend their Estates und'r Soe Leese and make a Govern-

m't and to yt end that yo'r Maj'ty may at all times have more particular Sattisfaction, and the persons concerned Oppertunitie upon Occaission further to Asserte and prove their interest withunto hazardinge their Orriginall Easements Apon the sea wee have caused an Oath to bee administered to our s'd Regester, under his hand to Attest all such deeds and papers as have bin received by us and to Copy and truly Examine the same and In like manner to Attest to Such Copies and afterwards to Retturne the Orriginalls and Copies upon Demand to ye parties yt Produced the same In Obedience to yo'r Maj'ties gracious Commission and Commands, wee with all humilitie Offer this o'r Report which wee Cause to be Duplicated, Concerneing yo'r Maj'ties graceous Acceptance of o'r Dutyfull Endeav'rs to Approve o'r Selves,

    Yo'r Maj'ties most Loyall and Obedient.
  Subjects,

Boston, Octob'r 20, 1683, Edward Cranfield,
           William Stoughton,
           Samuell Shrimpton,
           John Pynchon Juno'r,
           Nathaniel Saltonstall.

As a farther addition to o'r Reporte wee humbly offer that Since the close of yo'r Maj'ties Commission, mr. Edward Randolph arriveing and Signifieing his pow'r in behalfe of his Grace, ye Duke of Hamilton, to make Claime to the Kings Province or Narragansett Countrey, wee have againe Convened & Sumoned Soe many of the Proprieto'rs as could in Soe Short a time assemble, and in their presence and hearing heard read the Copie of the Dukes Deed and heard mr. Randolphs pleas and Improvements thereon & finde it takes in parte of the said Province or Narragansett Countrie, and have alsoe received the answ'rs and Defence of the said proprieto'rs which wee humbly transmitt and Submitt to yo'r Maj'ties Consideration, Wee have alsoe Ordered Copies of ye Dukes

Deeds and Propriet'rs Pleas to be sent to ye Colloney of Connecticott to the End, they maye have Oppertunie by the first Conveyance to make their answ'rs and Defence before y'or Maje'ty. Edward Cranfield,
William Stoughton,
Joseph Dudley.

Entered Upon Record, Nov'er 1st, 1686, P. John Fones Record'r.

(**43**) THIS INDENTURE of Exchange made and concluded upon the twenty sixth day of octob'r, Anno. Dom. one thousand six hundred ninty & seven Anno. qr Ke Ke Pulieb *Brinley and Viall's exchange.* Fortie anglia & nono., Betweene ffrancis Brinley of Newport on Rhod Island, in New England Merchant of the one part, and Samuell Vyall of Swansey in New England afores'd Yoeman on the other parte WITNESSETH that the said ffrancis Brinley HATH given, granted & Confirmed, and by these presents for himselfe, his heires DOTH fully, freely, clearly and absolutely give, grant & Confirme unto the said Samuell Vyall, his heires and Assignes for ever in Exchange Eighty nine Acres of Land Lying on Boston Neck, (soe called) in the Naraganset Country within the Kings Province in New England afores'd adjoyning to the Northermost part of the s'd Vyal, his farme Runing from Sea to Sea according as it is laid out by Robert Hazzard, Surveyor, TOGETHER with all priviledges, rights, commodities, heriditaments & appurtenances whatsoever to the said Land belonging or in any wise appertaining, And alsoe all the Estate, righte, title, Interest, inheritance, use, possession, reversetion, remainder, property, claimes & demand whatsoever of the s'd ffrancis Brinley and his heires of, in and to the Same & Every part thereof To HAVE & TO HOLD the said Eighty nine Acres of Land with the appurtenances before in these presants give, granted and confirmed unto Samuel Viall, his heires and assignes To the only Sole and proper use and behoofe of the Said Samuell Viall, and of his heires and assignes for ever, without the least lett, Suite, trouble, deniall, molestation, Eviction or ejection of the said ffrancis Brinley, his heires or assignes or any of them or by any others, through his or their means or procurement in any maner or wise, And this Indenture further Witnesseth that the Said Samuel Viall hath given, granted and confirmed and by these presents for himself and his heires DOTH fully, freely, clearly and absolutely give, grant and Confirme unto the Said ffrancis Brinley, his heires & assignes for Ever in Exchange for the afore mentioned Land, Eighty nine Acres of Land Lying on the Southermost part of the Said Vialls ffarm next adjoyning to the S'd Brinley's Land on Boston Neck afore s'd, and running from Sea to Sea according as it way Lately Laid out by the Said Robert Hazzard, Surveyor, Together with all proffitts, priviledges, rights, anodityes, hereditments and appurtenances whatsoever to the Said Land belonging or in any wise appurtaining And also all the Estate, right, title, Interest, inheritance, use, possession, reversetion, remainder property, claimes & demand whatsoever of the Said Samuel Viall and his heires of, in and to the same and Every part thereof, TO HAVE & TO HOLD the said Eighty nine Acres of Land with the appurtenances, lest before in these presents given, granted and confirmed unto the Said ffrancis Brinley his heires and assignes To the only Sole and proper use, benefit and behoofe of him the said ffrancis Brinley, his heires.

(44) and assignes for ever with't the least lett, Suite, trouble, deniall, molestotion, eviction or ejction of the Said Samuell Viall, his heires or assignes or any of them or by any others through his or their meanes or procurement in any maner or wise, IN WITNESS whereof the Said parties to these p'sent Indentures have hereunto Interchangeably sett their hand and Seale the day and year first above Written.
Signed, Sealed and Delivered
   in presence of us,   Francis Brinley,
   G. Syluesse,
   Elizabeth Huling.

Francis Brinley the within mentioned, appeared and acknowledged the within Instrum't to be his reall act & deed the 13th day of May, 1698.   Before John Fones, Assist. Entered upon Record the third
day of September, 1705.
P. Samuell Fones, Clerke of Kingstowne.

(49*) To all CHRISTIAN PEOPLE to whome these p'sents shall come, KNOW YE that whereas Coginaquand and Mossip Indian sachems did by their deed bearing date ye twenty seventh day of May in ye yeare of o'r Lord one thousand six hundred fifty and nine, Passe and convey to Randall Holding and Sam'l Gorton of warrick, a Tract or Neck of land in ye Narragansett countrey in wch is comprehended or contained a smaller Neck of land formerly called Nanequassett Al's Homogansett, Also a small Island neare ye same called Sawanoxs'tt and by ye English fox Island which s'd smaller Neck or Island Containing by Estimation one hundred & Eighty Acers more or less is bounded (viz.,) The said smaller Neck by ye land now belonging to William Taylor & Richard Wharton to ye westward, with ye land of mr. Richard Smith northward, To ye Eastward wth ye salt water and to ye southward wth ye salt water and at the ye head of ye S'd Neck with ye Brook or river comonly called Annaquatuckett Al's Annucktusick on ye South wchich s'd smaller Neck & Island here for above nine yeares last past been in ye occupation and possession of Robert Greene & Thomas Brookes as tennants to ye s'd Tailor & Wharton, Now I ye S'd Randall Holding for a valueable Consideration to mee in hand paid by the S'd William Tailor & Richard Wharton wherewith I acknowledge my selfe fully satisfied, doe by these p'sents Grant, bargaine, sell, aliene, demise, convey & confirme all my part, portion & Interest, right & title in and to ye said smaller Necke being bounded as afores'd (or however otherwise) as also all my part, portion, Interest & Title in and to s'd Island called fox Island, To them the s'd Wm. Tailor, Rich'd Wharton, their

---

* Pages 45, 46, 47, 48 are blank in the original manuscript.

heires & assignes for Ever to have & to hold all that my part, portion, Interest, right & title in and to ye S'd Necke of land & Island, Containing one hundred & Eighty Acres in ye whole, be the same more or less, Together wth all privilidges, benefits & Advantages to ye same belonging or in any wise appurtaining To them ye s'd William Tailor & Richard Wharton, their heires & Assignes for ever as a perfect, absolute & Indefeasable Estate, And I ye s'd Randall Holding doe also by these presents acquit for Ever, Acquit, Exonerate, discharge & fully release the s'd Tailor and Wharton, and all & every their tennants or other persons at any time Imployed by any of them from all damages, acts of intruesion or trespass, or any use or improvements, made, committed or done upon ye Premisses or any part thereof. And I doe further promis by these p'sents at all times hereafter to warrant & defend ye s'd William Tailor & Rich'd Wharton, their & every of their heires, Executo'rs, Administrato'rs or Assignes, from all persons claiming any Title, Interest or Dower in or to ye Premises, by, from or under mee. And in WITNESS hereof, I hereunto set my hand & seale this twenty fower day of November, An'o Dom Christi one thousand six hundred eighty & one, And in ye three & thirtieth yeare of his maj'ties Reigne.

Signed, sealed & delivered in Presence of

It is to be understood by all persons that shall construe, paragraph or Expound all any particular, contained in this deed of sale, that ye true intent & meaning is only one third part of ye whole tract of land mentioned, being the whole claime and interest of ye above said Randall Holding, as also doth acquit and discharge no further, but to his owne part, title or interest, his heires or Assignes (therefore explained before signeing & sealing to avoid mistakes.

Randall Holden,

Witness, Sam'll Gorton, Assistant,
Benjamin Gorton,
Thomas Gaddinton,

I ffrancis Houlding, wife of Randall Houlding, doe consent to ye deed of sale and for ever will quitt clayme; Witness my hand & Seale ye 12th day of May, 1682. The marke of
Witness, William Tanner,   ffrancis H. Houlding,
Peter Wells.

This deed was signed, sealed & delivered by Capt. Randall Houlding to mr. Rich'd Smith of Narragansett in behalfe of mr. Will'm Taylor & mr. Rich'd Wharton of Boston, merchant as Attest, Sam'l Gorton, Asist.

Rochester, June 24th, 1686, Richard Smith Esquire testifieth that he wrote ye Acknowledgement of ffrancis Holding, ye wife of mr. Randall Holding, and that he saw her signe ye same, as now ye same appeares on ye other syde, and voluntarily post ye same; And Peter wells, yeoman, saith upon oath, that he was also present and saw ye s'd ffrances Holding signe ye same, and as a witness he subscribed his marke which now appeares on ye other syde.

Sworne before me,   J. Dudley, Ps'd,

Entered upon Record June ye 26th, 1686,
P. Jno. Fones, Recorder.

To all Christian People to whome these Presents shall come, Know yee that Whereas Coginaquand and Mossip Indian *Wm. Maze to Wharton & Taylor* Sachems did by their Deed bearing date ye twenty seventh day of May in ye yeare of o'r lord, one thousand six hundred fifty & nine, sell and convey To mr. Randall Holdinge & mr. Sam'll Gorton of warwick, a Tract or Necke of land in ye Narragansett country, in which is Comprehended or contained a smaller Necke of land called formerly Nanequassett, Alias Homogansett, also a small Island neare ye same called Sowanoxett, and by ye English fox Island wch said smaller Necke or Island Containing by estimation one hundred and eighty Acres more or less is bounded (viz.,) ye s'd smaller necke by ye land now belonging to William Tailor & Rich'd Wharton To ye westward, with ye land of mr.

Rich'd Smith Northward, To ye Eastward wth ye salt water and to ye southward with ye salt water, And at ye head of ye s'd necke with ye Brooke or River comonly called Annaquatuckett Al's Annachatusick, on ye south which s'd smaller necke and Island have for above nine yeares last past been in ye occupation and possession of Robert Greene and Thomas Brookes as Tennants To ye s'd Tailor & Wharton, And forasmuch as I William Mayes, of Newport, in Rhode Island, and by virtue of a Guift from my wife's father ye s'd Sam'll Gorton as als by Purchase from John Crandall became intrusted in, and Proprietor off part of ye Premises ; Therefore, I, ye s'd William Mayes, for a valuable Consideration

(50) To me in hand paid by ye s'd Wm. Tailer & Rich'd Wharton wherewith I acknowledge myselfe fully satisfied, Doe by these Presents, Grant, bargaine, sell, Aliene, Demise, convey and Confirme all my part, portion & interest, right & Title, in & to ye s'd smaller Necke, being bounded as afores'd or however otherwise as also all my part, portion, Interest, right & Title, in, and to ye s'd Island called ffox Island, To them, ye s'd William Tailer & Richard Wharton, their heires & Assignes for ever, To have & to hold all that my part, porton, Interest, right & title in and to ye s'd necke of land & Island, Containing one hundred and eighty Acres in ye whole, be ye same more or less, Together wth all privilidges, benifits and advantages to ye same belonging, or in any wise appertaining To them ye s'd William Taylor & Richard Wharton, their heires & Assignes for ever as a good, perfect, absolute and Indefeasable Estate in fee simple, And I, ye s'd William Mayes, doe also by these presents for ever acquit, Exonerate, discharge & Release the s'd Tailer & Wharton, and all & every their Tennants or other persons at any time imployed by any of them, from all Damages, acts of Intrusion or Trespesses, or any use or Improvements made, Comitted, or done upon ye Premisses or any part thereof; And I doe

further promise by these Presents at all times hereafter to warrant & defend the s'd William Tailer & Rich'd Wharton, their & every of their heires, Executo'rs, Administrato'rs & Assignes, from all P'sons claiming any Title, interest or Dower, in or to ye Premises by, from or under me, And in Witness hereof I hereunto set my hand & seale, this twenty third day of November, An'o Dom Christi, one thousand six hundred Eighty & one, and in ye three & thirtieth yeare of his Majesty's Reigne,

William Maze seale.

Sealed & delivered in presence of his /M\ marke.

Francis Brinley, Lott Strainge,
Robert Hazsard, Simon Grover.

I Sarah Mayes doe consent to ye above written Deed, and every quitt Claime for me and my heires, To ye s'd William Tailer & Richard Wharton, their heires & Assignes for ever.

Sarah X Mayes
her marke.

Rochester, June 24, 1686, Wm. Maze P'sonally apeared before me, the subscriber being one of his majes'tirs Councill, and acknowledged this Instrum't to be his voluntary act & deed.   J. Winthrop.

Rochester, June 24, 1686, francis Brinley P'sonally opeared and made oath yt he saw Will'm Maze and Sarah Maze his wife, seal, deliver & acknowledge ye Deed within, and that he ye deponant at ye time thereof subscribed his name as a Witness Thereto.
Sworne before me.   J. Dudley, P'sd.

Entered upon Record June 26, 1686.
    Jno. Fones, Recorder.

Know all men that I Samuell Cranston of Newport, on Rhode Island, for a Considerable value in hand received from

Samuel Cranston and Mary Jones to Wharton, Esq'r. Richard Smith of Narragansett in the Kings Province, doe by these Presents, sell, make over and convey all my right and Title in a small Necke of land Called Homogansett, with my right in a small Island called annoxett Al's fox Island, wch land was conveyed & given to my father by Samuell Gorton & Capt. Randall Houlding, By Cogiquant or Tasaquonet sould or given to them in may 27th day 1659, this Necke & Island being now in ye occupation of Thomas Brookes Tennant to mr. Richard Wharton, merchant in Boston, this Necke & Island being but part of my right, haveing sould all ye rest of my right without, and my other Necke caled Nanaquaxett or Al's Kesoconico unto Rich'd Smith aforesaid before ye ensealing hereof, I say, I sell & make over this s'd Necke Homogansett and fox Island unto mr. Rich'd Wharton, his heires and Assignes for ever, all my right, Title I have or ought to have free of all dower Jointures or intailes or Incumbrances whatsoever by me made, had or done, And doe warrant it free of all manner of Challeng, Claime or Incumberance by reason of any right of my deceased father, major John Cranston, In Witness hereof, I have set my [hand] and seale and by Consent of my Mother, Mrs. Mary Jones, being my voluntary act and Deed and for a valueable Consideration as above Exprest this 11th of April, 1685,

Samuell Cranston &   seale

Mary   Jones, &   seale

her marke

I, Mary Jones, above Exprest do concent to ye above Deed of sale and do for ever quit my claime.

Signed, Sealed & Delivered in ye Presence of P. Francis Brinley, Walter Stephens Jun., P. Francis Brinley Esq, P'sonally appeared and made oath that he saw Sam'll Cranston & Mary Jones, Seale & Deliver ye deed above written as their volentary act & deed, and that he saw mr. Walter Stephens ye other Witness, thereof at ye same time being about ye day of ye date thereof subscribed his name as Witness Thereto. Sworn before me, J. Dudley, P'nt.

(51) To all Christian People unto whome these presents shall come, James Russell Esq. the onely surviving son, and Executo'r of ye last will & Testament Richard Russell Esq., *James Russell to Esq'r. Wharton.* Sometime of Charlestown in ye County of Miss'r within his Majes'ties Territory and Dominion of New England, in America sendeth Greeting, Know ye tha[t] I the said James Russell, for and in Consideration of ye sume of one hundred & fifty pounds current Money of New England, to me at ye ensealing & delivery of these Presents securred in ye law to be paid by Richard Wharton of Boston, within ye Territory & Dominion afores'd, Esq'r wherewith, I doe acknowledge my selfe well satisfied and contented, Have therefore granted, enfeefed, released, set over, Assigned, conveyed and Confirmed, and by these Presents do fully, freely and absolutely grant, Enfeefe, release, assigne, set over, convey & Confirme unto ye s'd Richard Wharton, his heires & Assignes for ever, all that my Messuage & Tenement and ye lands thereto adjourning, scituate, lying & being in ye Narragansett Country, within ye Territory & dominion afores'd, Containing all that farme formerly in ye occupation of Rob't Greene, as also the Necke of land neare adjoyning, thereunto containing by Estimation two hundred & fifty acres more or Less, sould by mr. Rich'd Smith unto Capt. William hudson of Boston, Vintner, all wch premisses were alienated and conveyed by ye said William Hudson, Together with all other lands and interests to him in any wise due and belonging within ye bonds of ye s'd Narragansett Country or lands there Ajacent, unto ye above named Richard Russell by Deed bearing date Octob'r 25, 1672, Excepting onely out

of ye s'd Sale such part of ye s'd Premisses as was mortgaged by ye said Hudson unto William Hutchinson of London, merchant, to ye value of about one hundred & fifty pounds sterling, wch is likewise hereby excepted, all other the s'd lande & rights conveyed unto ye s'd Rich'd Russell are hereby released unto ye s'd Rich'd Wharton part thereof in his actuall possession now being, Also all my Estate, right, Title interest use property, possession, claime and demand whatsoever of, in and unto ye same or to any part or parcell thereof, To have & to hold ye s'd Messuage, Tenem't and farme, necke of land and all other ye above granted Premisses Except as is above Excepted with ye rights, liberties, privilidges & apurtenances, thereto belonging unto him ye s'd Rich'd Wharton, his heires & assignes, To his & their onely proper use, behoofe and benefitt for ever, free & clear & freely Exonerated, acquited & discharged of & from all and all manner of former and other Gifts, grants, sales, releases, assignments, Titles, claimes, troubles, charges, acts and Incumbrances whatsoever had made, done, comitted or suffered to be done by ye s'd Rich'd Russell or me ye s'd James Russell, or by o'r or either of o'r meanes, act, assent, default, consent, Title or procurement, And further I ye s'd James Russell doe covenant, promise, bynd and oblige my selfe, my heires, Executo'rs & Administrato'rs to warrant, maintaine, uphold and defend all & every ye above granted premisses unto ye s'd Rich'd Wharton, his heires & assignes forever against my selfe, my heires, Executo'rs & Administrato'rs and against every of ye heires, of ye s'd Rich'd Russell, and all & every other person and persons, whomsoever lawfully haveing'c[l]aming or pretending to have or claime any right, Title, interest ord demand in or to ye same or to any part or parcell thereof from, by or under us, any or either of us.

In Witness whereof, I, ye s'd James Russell have hereunto sett my hand & seale this nineteenth day of June, Ano Dom one thousand six hundred Eighty & six Ano Regini Regis Jacobi Anglia secundo. James Russell & seale.

Signed, Sealed & Delivered
  in ye presents of us.
    Elisha Hutchinson,
      John Saffin,

Boston, ye 19th of June, 1686.

James Russell Esq., ye within named,
Grantor acknowledged this Instrument to be his act & Deed before me under written, one of his majes'ties Councill, in ye Territory & Dominion of New England in America.
                              Wait Winthrop.
This Deed Entered upon Record June 28th, 1686.
              P. Jno. Fones, Record'r.

(**52**) To all Christian people to whome these presents shall come; Know yee That I Richard Smith, of Nara'set, in the King's province in New England, Esq., for divers good causes and Consideration mee thereunto moveing Especially _{Smith to Wharton.} for that Respect and friendship I beare to Richard Wharton of Boston, Esq'r, and the greate desire I have to promote the good Settle'mt of this Towne, have given, granted, Released, aliened, Enfeefed and confirmed, and doe by these presents give, grant, Release, alien, Enfeeffe and confirme to him the said Richard Wharton, all that peace or parcell of Land aboute fourteene months since Surveyed by mr. John Gore, and marked and Laid out to the said Richard Wharton, being bounded Southerly by Annogatuckett River, and northerly by the highway leading to Jacob Pinder's, Containing aboute twenty seven Acres, be the same more or less, howsoever the same may bee, although butted or Bounded After full and free Libertie upon my land in the occupation of the s'd Jacob Pindor, where maye bee most convenient, and in, upon and throught the s'd River of Annogatucket to Erect, Build and make a dam for Mill or Mills, and to raise the water upon my Land Soe farr as maye bee need full to make a pond or head to Supply and drive Such Mill or Mills as may bee

Erected on the Said Stream, or any flumes or *Townes* that maye bee drawed from the same, Alsoe soe much Land on ye northern side of Annogatuckett River, is maye bee needfull to sett the Mill or Mills upon, if the same shall bee found more conven't then the said Whartons Land Adjoining together, wth the Libertie of a highway to Such Mill or Mills, To have and to hold the aforesaid piece or parcele of Land Containing twenty seven Acres more or less, and the full and free libertie, use and Sale, benefitt of land for Dam or Dams and Mill poole or ponds, and Land as afore s'd for Mill or Mills together wth the Liberty of highway and free Egress and Regress as maye bee need full through the Land in the occupation of the said Jacob Pindar, To him the S'd Rich'd Wharton, his heires and assignes for Ever, and I, the S'd Richard Smith doe hereby Covenante and grant to and wth the said Richard Wharton, his heires & assignes, That hee and they shall and maye by virtue of these presents, for ever peaceably and quietly possess and Enjoye the premisses, and Every part and parcell thereof, and all privilidges granted and needfull to ye Same, a good, P'fect and Indefeaseable Estate of Inheritance without any manner of Lett, Denyall, Trouble or molestation from mee the S'd Richard Smith or Hester my wife, or any P'son or P'sons claimeing By, from or und'r us or Either of us, In Witness whereof I, the said Richard Smith together wth Hester, my wife, have hereunto putt o'r hands and Seales this twenty Eighte day of June, one thousand six hundred Eighty six, and in the Second yeare of the Raigne of o'r Soveraignes Lord King James the Second.   Rich'd Smith, & a Seale.
                 Hester Smith, & a Seale.

Sealed and Dellevered June 28th, 1686.
In presence of Francis Brinley,
    Elisha Hutchinson,
    John Saffin,

maj'r Rich'd Smith acknowledged, In Open Courte the

above written Instrum't to bee his reall acte & deed, and was by said Courte ordered to bee placed to Record as Attest.

John Fones, Clerke.

Entered upon Record, June the 28th, 1686.
P.   Jno. Fones, Record'r.

This indenture made the Six and twentieth daye of May, in the yeare of o'r Lord one thousand Six hundred Sixty Six, in the Eighteenth yeare of ye Raigne of o'r Soveraigne Lord Charles ye Second, by the grace of God, of England, Scotland, *Fowler to Clarke.* france and Island King &c, Betweene Henry ffowler of providence, in New England, Blacksmith, on the one syde; and Thomas Clarke of Boston, in the County of Suffolke, in New England, Merchant, in the other Part, witnesseth, that the said Henry ffowler for and in Consideration of the Sum of fortie pounds of currant Money in New England, to him in hand before the Sealeing and Deliverery hereof, well and truely pay'd by the above named Thomas Clarke, whereof and wherewith the sayd Henry ffowler doth acknowledge himselfe to bee fully Sattisfied, contented and pay'd, and thereof and of Every part and P'sell thereof doth Clearely and absolutely acquitt & discharge the Sayd Thomas Clarke, his heires, Executo'rs, administrat'rs and assignes, and every of them for ever by these P'sents hath given, granted, Bargained, Sealed, aliened,

(**53**) Enfeeffed and Confirmed, and by these P'sents doeth fully, Clearly & absolutely give, grant, Bargaine, Selle, alien, enfeeffe and Confirmed unto the Said Thomas Clarke, his heires and assignes for Ever, a P'sell of Land lyeing and being at ye mouth or Entrance of pettewomuck River, in ye Naragansett Country, Containeing one hundred and fifty acres, bee it more or Less, and is butteing on the Said pettewomuck River, Northerly, and on the Land of Thomas Gold, Southerly, and is Bounded by the Bay of Narragansett, Easterly, and by the Land of Caleb Carr, Westerly, wth all woods, waies, Commons, proffits, Commodities, priviledges and Appurtenances whatsoever to the S'd P'cell of land bellonging, or in any wise appurtaineing, and all ye Estate, righte, title, interest, use, property, possession, Claime and Demand whatsoever, of him the said Henry ffowler, of, in or to the Same or any part thereof, and deeds, writeings or Evidences whatsoever toucheing or concerneing the primesses or any part thereof, to have and to hold the Sayd P'cell of land wth the privilidges & appertenances to ye s'd Thomas Clarke, his heires & assignes forever, to & for ye use & behoofe of ye s'd Thos. Clarke, his heires & assignes for ever, & the s'd Henry ffowler, for himselfe, his Executo'rs Administrat'rs doe, Covenant, promise & grante to the s'd Thos. Clarke, vt ye above named land conveyed as above s'd from henseforth shall be and continue unto the S'd Thos. Clarke, his heires & assignes a Cleare and free discharge and acquitted or otherwise from tyme to tyme and at all tymes upon Request Sufficiently Served and Replevened of and from all & all manner of former & other gifts, grants, Bargains, Salles, Leases, assignm'ts, mortgaged, wills, entailes, Judgm'ts, Executions, fofetures, Dowers, power of thirds of Rebecka, his now wife, to bee Claimed or Challenged of in or to ye same or parte thereof, & of and from all and singular other Charges, Rents, titles, troubles, incumbrances and Demands whatsoever had, made or done, occassioned or Suffered to bee, done by the sayd Henry Fowler or any other P'son or P'sons whatsoever by his or their act or means, default, Consent or Procurement, and that the Sayd Thomas Clarke, his heires & assignes the Sayd Bargained, premisses, with ye privilidges and appurtenances there to Bellonging, Shall and maye from henseforth for ever peaceably have, use, possess, occupie and enjoye to his and their own proper use, and behoofe withoute ye lett, Suite, trouble, molestation, deniall, eviction, ejection or disturbance of the said Henry Fowler, his heires, Executo'rs, administrato'rs or any other P'son or P'sons whatsoever Lawfully Claimeing or pretending to have any Estate, right, title, interest, Claime or demand whatsoever of, in or to the Same or any parte thereof in, by or through him, In witness whereof the Sayd Henry Fowler and Rebecka his wife have hereunto sett their hands and Seales the day and yeare first above written.

his marke.

Henry H̄F̄ Fowler & a seale.
Rebecka Fowler   seale.

Signed & Sealed in P'sence of us,

John Parmitter.
John Sayles.

This twenty seventh of June, One thousand Six hundred Sixty and Six, Henry Fowler and Rebecka, his wife, owne the above written, their act and deede in the p'sence of us.

William Carpenter, Assist't.
William Harris, Assist't

of the Jurisdiction of Rhoad Island and providence plantations &c.

he above written deede is placed to Record in the booke of Records bellonginge to the Colony of Rhoad Island in the 316 page thereof, November the 11th, 1669.

Pr. me   Joseph Torrey, Gen'll Record'r.

Rochester, June ye 28th, 1686.
this deed is alowed to bee Recorded.

Rich'd Wharton.

Entered upon Record, June ye 28th, 1686.
P. Jno. Fones, Record'r.

To all Christian People to whome this present Instruem't shall Come, Capt. Thomas Clarke of Boston, in the Collony of the Massachusetts in New England, merchant, send- *Clarke to Hudson.* eth Greeting in o'r Lord God Everlasting, Whereas Henry Fowler, of providence in New England, Blacksmith, and Rebecka his wife, by their deed of Sale, bearing date the Six and twentieth day of May in the yeare of o'r Lord, one thousand Six hundred Sixty and Six, hath given, granted, Bargained, Sold, aliened, Enfeoffed & Confirmed unto Thomas Clarke of Boston, in New England, merchant, his heires and assignes for ever, a peece or P'cell of land Lyeing and being at ye mouth or Entrance of petewomuck River in the Narragansett Country, Containing one hundred and fiftie Acres, bee it more or Lesse, and is Butting and Bounded as by the deede of Sale thereof before Recited, refference thereto being had more fully appeareth, Now know yee that the said Capt. Thomas Clarke for and in Consideration of the Sume of forty and five pounds in mony Currant in New England, to him in hand before the Sealeing and Dellivery hereof well and truely payd by Capt. Wm. Hudson of Boston aforesaid, vinttner, the receipt which The Said Thomas Clarke doth acknowledge by these presents and therewith to bee fully

(54) Satisfied and Contented, and thereof, and of every part and P'cell thereof doth acquitt and discharge the Said Wm. Hudson, his heires, Executo'rs, administrato'rs & assignes and every of them for ever by these presents hath given, granted, Bargained, Sould, aliend, assigned and Sett over, and by these presents doth fully, Freely and absolutely give, grante, Bargaine, alien, assigne & Sett over unto the Said Wm. Hudson, his heires and assignes for ever as well the Said P'cell of land together wth the proffits, privilidges and appertenances thereof, and there to Bellonging according to the teno'r of the above Recited deed of Sale, together wth the same deed of Sale, and alsoe the Estate, right, title, interest, use, propriety, possession, claime and demand whatsoever wch hee ye s'd Thomas Clarke, his heires or assignes, now hath or in any wise maye, might should or ought to have, of, in or to ye premisses by force and virtue of the above Recited deed of Sale, to have and to hold the said Bargained Sould and assigned premisses unto the s'd William Hudson, his heires & assignes, to his and their owne

proper use and Behoofe for ever, free and cleere, and hereby acquitted and Discharged of and from all, and all maner of former, and other gifts, grantes, Bargaines, Sales, Assign'mt and acts of incumbrances, whatsoever had made, done or Suffered to bee done by the s'd Thomas Clarke, his heires, Executo'rs, administrato'rs or any other P'son or P'sons whatsoever Lawfully claimeing or to claime any Estate, Right, title, interest, claime or demand whatsoever, of, in or to ye Same or any part Thereof, from, by or und'r him or them, any or either of them, whereby the Said Wm. Hudson or his heires or assignes, Shall or maye bee at any time hereafter molested in Evicted from the Lawfull and peaceable possession thereof, IN WITNESS whereof The S'd Thomas Clarke hath hereunto Sett his hand and Seale, the one & twentieth day of novemb'r in the yeare of o'r Lord, one thousand Six hundred Sixty & Six, Anno qr Regine Regis Caroly Secondi XVIII.

Thomas Clarke & a Seale.

Signed, Sealed and Delivered
in the presence of us.
John Viall,
William Pearse Sr.

the above written deed is placed to Record in the Gen'll booke bellonging to ye Collony of Rhoad Island, and in the (317) page thereof, novemb'r 12th, 1669.

P. mee Joseph Torrey, gen'll Record'r.

Rochester, June 28th, 1686.

This deed is allowed to bee Record'd.

Richard Wharton.

Entered upon Record June 29, 1686.
P. Jno. Fones, Record'r

Know all men by these presents, that I, Capt. Wm. Hudson, of Boston, in New England, doe by these Presents from *Hudson to Tibits.* mee, my heires & assignes, make over, Bargaine and Sell unto Henry Tibbetts of Narragansett, his heires, Executo'rs, Administrato'rs and assignes in and for full consideration to mee given and by mee Received, all my right, title, and interest in One hundred and fifty acres of land, bee it more or lesse, which land was Sould by Henry Fowler To Capt. Thomas Clarke of Boston, merchant, as maye appeare by a deed beareing date the twenty sixth of May, in the yeare of o'r Lord God, one thousand Six hundred Sixty and Six, and in the Eighteenth yeare of the reigne of o'r Sovereigne Charles Second of England, Scotland, france and Ireland, as alsoe by an other deed beareing date the one and twentieth day of Novemb'r, one thousand Six hundred Sixty and Six, under the hand and Seale of Thomas Clarke, of Boston afore s'd as more at Large maye appeare by the foresaid deeds, now know yee to whom these presents

(55) Shall come, that I, william Hudson aforesaid, doe by these presents, in Consideration as for above s'd, doe fully, freely, absolutely make over, Bargaine and Sell from mee my heires and assignes, all my right, title and interest in the aboves'd Lands unto Henry Tibets, his heires and assignes for ever, peacably to Enjoy as his and their proper right and interest the S'd Lands butteing on Potowomuck River, Northerly, and upon ye Lands of mr. Thomas Gould, Southerly, and by Narragansett Bay, Easterly, and by the Land formerly Caleb Carr's, westerly, all which lands wth in the said Bounds contained, I doe sell as above s'd with all the woods, meadows, Commons, privilidges or appurtainces there unto bellonging or appurtaineing, I not Reserveing any wife's Dowry or Joynture, acknowledging by these pres'nts to have putt ye Said Henry Tibbitts in full and ample possession of all & every parcell of ye primisses above s'd, and doe promise the same to defend from any Layeing Claimes to any of the primisses in my name or by my means, cause or consent whatsoever, in Witness whereof, I the above s'd Wm Hudson hath hereunto Sett his hand and Seale this twentie Eight of February, one thousand Six hundred Sixty and Seven, and in the nineteenth yeare of ye raigne of o'r Soveraigne Lord Charles

the Second of England, Scotland, france and Ireland King.

Will Hudson & a Seale.

Signed, Sealed and Delivered in
    the presence of us.
    Rich'd Smith,
        his marke,

    Samuel   Eldred,
        his marke.

    Thomas   Sewell,

The above written deed is placed to Record in the booke of Records bellonging to the Collony of Rhoad Island and in the (317) page thereof.
        P. mee Joseph Torrey, Gen'll Record'r.
Rochester, June 28th, 1686.
Maj'r Richard Smith and Thomas Sewell appeared in open Courte, and did declare upon Oath, they did see Capt. Wm. Hudson, Seale, acknowledge and Deliver the above written deed of Sale, and did Subscribe their names as Witnesses, Thereto as Attest:
Jno. Fones, Clerke.

Entered upon Record June 29th 1686.
P.   Jno. Fones, Record'r.

    Newport the 3d of ye 7th month Soe called 1651.
This writeing testifieth that I, Rog'r Williams of Providence, for and in Consideration of fifty pounds already received have Sould and Demised unto mr. Rich'd Smith of *Williams to Smith.* portsmouth on Road Island, his heires & assignes for ever, my tradeing house at Narragansett, together with two Iron Guns or murderers, there Lyeing as alsoe my fields & fenceing aboute the s'd House, is alsoe the use of the litle Island for goates which the old Sachem, deceased, Lent mee

for that use, for confirmation of all which I Sett my hand & Seale ye daye and yeare aforesaid.

Roger Williams & a seale.

In the presence of
Thomas Newton,

Jeffere   *his mark*   Champlain,

John   *his mark R*   Roome,

William   *his mark WH*   Holmes,

Rochester, June 28th, 1686.
The writeing within is alowed to bee Recorded.

R'd Wharton.

Entered upon Record June 29th, 1686.
P. Jno. Fones, Record'r.

Bee it knowne unto all men yt I, Tasaquanat alias Cogina- *Cojinaquand to Smith* quand, chiefe Sachem of the Narragansett Country, doe by these presents for and in Consideration of full Sattisfaction in hand, given and received from Rich'd Smith Sen'r and Rich'd Smith Jun'r, doe by these presents give, grant and Lease out unto the fores'd Richards, their heires and assignes, a certain tract of Land for the full

(**56**) and compleate tearme of Sixty yeares, the land being sittuated, to the Southward of the now dwelling house [hadeing (sic)] at Potomcasutt, It being bounded on the northwest by the English path or common Rhoad waye that goeth to poquitt, as farr as anochetuckett River, on the south and southwest bounded by anochetuckett river, and on the southeast bounded by the maine bay, or Broad watters, on the northeast and north by Potomcosutt Harbour, and Soe to ye fore s'd path or comon Rodewaye aforesaid, all which lands, meadows, Neckes of land or other privilidges within there afore s'd

Bounds contained, I the aforesaid Sachem doe rent and Lease Out Absolutely and valluntairly for the term of three score or Sixty yeares as above s'd, I haveing already received Sattisfaction in hand for the whole tearme of yeares pay'd mee as Rent, alsoe I doe ingage that noe Indian Shall plant within the foresaid tract of Land dureing the foresaid term of yeares above s'd and that the said tract of land Shall bee at ye use and dispose of the s'd Richards Smiths, their heires & assignes during the terme, and doe here promise the Same to defend and mentaine their rights theirin, dureing the s'd terme of Sixty yeares, and further, I the s'd Tasaquanett alias Coginiquand have given my said tenants full and ample possession of the s'd tract of land, in witness of all above wretten, I binde my Selfe, my heires & assignes firmely by these presents and sett to my marke this Eighth day of march, 1656. alias.

The marke of Tasaquanett  Cogiquand.

This deed was Signed & Delivered
in ye presence of us,

marke
Samuel Waite, interpreter.

marke
Ruben Willis, interp'r.

marke
Mattaickis Indian interp'r.

Samuel Waight aged aboute 22 yeares, and Ruben Willis aged aboute 26 yeares, being both witnesses to this deed, made Oath before me, Daniel Gookin, majistrate of the Massachusetts, this 23d day of June, 1662, that they did see this deed Signed, delivered by Tasiquanett alias Cogiquand as his free Act, the contents thereof being fully made knowne unto him.

Coram mee   Daniel Gookin.

Entered and Recorded in the (316) page of the third booke of Records, of the Nottaries publick of the Massachusetts collony of New England, the 30th day of June Anno. 1662.

    P.   Robert Howard, nottary pub., Collinia, P'di'cs.

Ruben Willis, aged aboute 31 yeares, being ingaged testifieth this 13th of June, 1667, yt the deed on the other side hereof (that is to saye of this paper,)was Signed by Tasaquanitt alias Coginaquand, and dellivered by him to the said mr. Rich'd Smith Senio'r and mr. Rich'd Smith Junio'r, according as it is Expressed in the writeing on the other side, and accordinge to his Oath taken, (as there Expressed) alsoe the abovesaid testimoney taken the day and yeare abovesaid.

P. mee   Wm. Harris, assist.

Samuel Waight, aged 27 years or there abouts, upon Ingagem't this 26th 7'ber, 1667, witnesseth yt hee, ye said Samuel, was witness to ye deed on the other side, and That ye said Deed was interpreted unto and that then the said Sachem viz., Tasaquanitt alias Cojaniquand did signe and delliver as Expressed on the other Side hereof, & did make Oath as within Expressed, taken before mee, Wm. Carpenter, assist.

This deed on the other side & the above written are Entered in the pub. Records of ye Collony of Conecticutt, Lib. I, fol. 91, Aprill 18, 1679.

P.   John Allyn, Secret'y.

Rochester, June the 28th, 1686.

The deed and Testimonies aforegoing are allowed to bee Recorded in the Booke of this Province.

R'd Wharton.

Entered upon Record, June 29, 1686.

P. Jno. Fones, Recorder.

(**57**) Bee it Knowne unto all men by these pres'nts, that I, Coginiquand Cheife Sachem of the Narragansett, for divers considerations mee hereunto moveing, have Bargained, *Cojinaquand to Smith's.* Rented, Lett and Leased out for the term of One thousand yeares, too morrow, a Certaine P'cell of Land and meadows unto Rich'd Smith Senio'r of Cocomcosutt and unto Rich'd Smith Junio'r his Sonn, the lands and Meadows being Sittuated and bounded as follows, viz., from a small maple tree on the Northwest side of the tradeing house, by a spring on a Straight line to a greate high Rocky hill Lyeing Southwestly, from thence on a west lyne to a fresh river called by the name of anachatuckett on the South west Side, Bounded by the Said river and Soe to the path that goeth to Namocoke and from thence bounded by a greate neck on the South East and a path yt goeth to a Little river called Shawatuckquese and then bounded on the Southeast by the creek and and Soe round to Cocomcosutt harbour, and So to the river and Maple tree aforesaid, as alsoe all ye meadows at paquinapange and at Sawgoe and on the head and Sides of the northward cricks from the house, as alsoe a necke of land beareing Eastward from the house on the other Side of the Cone, part of which Neck is already inclosed, all which P'cells of land & meadows, I the Said Coginiquant, doe hyer out and grant this Least of for the full terme of On [e] Thousand yeares, to Morrow, to both the for s'd Richards Smiths, their heires and assignes, peaceably to Enjoy the Same, for which the fore s'd Rich'ds Smiths, their heires or Assignes is to pay on every mid sumer day a Red honney Suckell grasse, If it bee lawfully demanded for acknowledgem'ts; alsoe their pres'ts witness that I, Coginequand have putt these my these my S'd tenants in full & ample possession of ye fore s'd P'cells of land and meadows by the dellivery of itt into their hands at ye Syneing and Sealeing hereof, witness my hand this Eiaght of June, 1659.

his marke.

Coginiquand 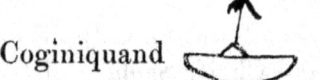 & a Seale.

Witness at ye Signeing, Sealeing
and dellivered of the same.
    marke
 Awashows ———*Ð* his
 Gysbert op dyck,
 James Smyth,
   his marke
 Ruben   Willis,
 Hester Smith,

Ruben Wiilis, aged 26 yeares, being a witness to this deed, made Oath before mee Daniel Gookin, assistant in the Massachusetts, that he did see Coginiquand, Signe, Seale and Delliver this lease and deed, and yt hee understood the contents thereof, Hester Smith acknowledges and affirmed that She was alsoe a witness to the same thing.

Before mee,   Daniel Gookin.

Entered and Recorded in the 316 & 317 pages of the third booke of Records of the nottary pub. of the Massachusetts collony of New England, the 30th day of June, anno 1662.

P.   Robert Howard not. pub. Cod'a P'ds.

Rochester, June 28th, 1686.

Allowed to be Recorded,   R'd Wharton.

Ruben Willis, Aged 31 yeares, thereabouts, testifieth this 13th of June, 1667, that according to the Oath and witness of his the Said Ruben Willis on the other Side of this paper written hee doth Still witness that hee did see Coginiquand, Signe, Seale & delliver the S'd writteing tomr. Rich'd Smith Senio'r and mr. Rich'd Smith Junio'r, testified upon his Engagem't before mee.

Wm. Harris, assist.

The deed on the other Side and the above written is Entered in the publick Records of the Collony of Connecticutt, Lib. 1st, folo. 91, Aprill the 18th, 1679.

P. John Allyn, Secretarey.

Rochester, June 28th, 1686.
This testimoney is allowed to be Recorded.

R'd Wharton.

Entered upon Record, June 29th, 1686.

P. Jno. Fones, Record'r.

(58) Bee it Knowne unto all men by these pres'ts, that I, Co-^{Cojinaquand to Smith.}giniquand, Cheife Sachem of Narragansett, for and in Consideration of my great love and affection I beare to Englishmen, wth divers Considerations mee hereunto moveing have given & granted unto Richard Simith Junio'r, now Resid't at Cocomcosutt a small Island Sittuated and Lyeing in Cocomcosutt Harbour, on the South East Side of the Tradeing house which S'd Island I doe give and grant to the fore s'd Rich'd Smith, his heirs and assignes for ever, to enjoye the same, and doe promis & engage to defend it and mentayne it to bee his and their proper rights for ever, and have given him full & ample Possession of all and Singular this my Said Island, by the delivery of it all in his hand at the signeing and Sealeing hereof, in wittness of the Same, I have Sett my hand and Seale this 27th of June, 1659.

his marke of

Cogoniquand  Sachem.

Sealed, Signed and Delivered
  in the presence of us.
    Gysbert ap Dyck,
    Hester Smith,

The above written deed is entered in the publick Records of the collony of conecticutt, Aprill 18th, 1679.

P. John Allyn, Secret.

Rochester, June 28th, 1686.

The above written deed is alowed to bee Recorded in the Booke of This Province.

R'd Wharton.

Entered upon Record June 29th, 1686.

P. Jno. Fones, Record'r.

Know all men by these pres'ts, that I, Scuttube & Quequaganewett, Sons of Mixon, late deceased, and chiefe Sachem of the Narragansett Country, doe by these presents Rattifie and *Scuttub & Quequaganuet to Smiths.* Confirm a certain tract of land to ye Northward of Cocumcosutt, now being given to mr. Richard Smith senio'r, By o'r father Mexcon afore s'd, the land being bounded as followeth, from a Maple tree on the northwest Syde of the tradeing house, north Easterly as farr alongst the English path as the head of a Small meadow, and so downe to ye Syde of a Creeck, being bounded by the watter or Pond to ye Eastward, alsoe Soe Rounde to ye Sayd maple tree aforesaid, bounded by watter, alsoe, wee the foresaid, Scuttub and Quequaganewett doe confirme and Rattifie all other grantes or leases made to Rich'd Smith, Senio'r, and to Rich'd Smith, Junio'r, to be as firme and Authentick as if o'r Selves had Signed the Same, as namely, two being made by Coginiquand, and one to Rich'd Smith, Junio'r, for a litle Island made by Coginiquand, all wich wee doe by these pres'ts rattifie and confirme, the one being for one thousand yeares to Morrow, the other being a deed of gift, ye litle Island, the other a necke of land Leased out for Sixty yeares, which Sayd necke, wee Scuttub and Quequaganewett, doe by these presents vallentairelly, freely and absolutely give to Rich'd Smith, Senio'r, Rich'd Smith, Junio'r, to them, their heires and assignes for ever, to enjoye the same, Itt being by inheritance o'r proper rights and interests, and, therefore, noe other Sachim can make good Sale of any part or P'cell of this fore said neck without o'r Rattification of the Same, this necke being bounded on the Southwest by Anochetuckett River, On the northwest by Namocock, south on ye north by Shewotuck Creeke, on the south and Sonth East by the main Bay or broad watter, all which lands according to the Contents above said deeds, Leases, instruements of writeing made to ye Said Richard Smith, Senio'r, and Rich'd Smith Junio'r, they or either of them wee doe Rattifie and Confirme and mentaine to Stand in full Strength, force and virtue, and doe promis the Same to mentaine against any Layeing claime to it or any of the premisses above s'd to the truth hereof, wee bynde o'r Selves, o'r heires and assignes, and Sett to our hands

(59) and Seales this 12th octob'r, 1660.

the marke of

Scuttub   & a Seale.

the marke of

Quequaganewett   & a Seale,

Wittnessess hereunto,

Powetuck ✗ Indian,

the marke of

Ruben Willis,

the marke of

Samuel Waight,

This writeing together wth the Endorse'mt is Entered and Recorded in the 317 & 318 pages of the third booke of Records of the Not'ry Pub. of the Massachusetts Colonie of New England, the 30th day of June, Anno 1662.

P. Robert Howard, no't. pub. Coloni, P'dit

Samuell Waight, aged aboute 22 yeares, and Ruben Willis, aged aboute 26 yeares, being wittnesses unto ye deed within written, made Oath before mee Daniel Gookin, magistrate of the Jurisdiction of Massachusetts, this 23th of June, 1662, that they were wittnesses hereunto, and did see Scuttub and Quequaganewett Signie and Seale the said writeing, the contents thereof being first made Known to them.

Jurater Cora mee, Daniel Gookin,

Ruben Willis, aged abought 31 yeares, being engaged, testifieth this 13th of June, 1667, that the deed written on ye other side of this paper was Signed by Scuttub and Quequaganewett, and by them Sealed and dellivered to mr. Rich'd Smith, Senio'r, and mr. Rich'd Smith, Junio'r, and accordinge to his oath above said before, mr. Daniel Gookin testifieth the day and yeare before [written]

[Before] mee William Harris, assist.

Samuel Waight, aged 27 yeares or thereabouts, and Engaged this 26th of Sept., 1667, testifieth that hee ye said Samuel was witness to the deed on the other side, and Saw Scuttub and Quequaganewett, Sigine and Seale ye Same, the contents first being made Knowne to the Said Scuttub and Quequaganewett; and yt hee, ye Said Samuel did make & take Oath as above S'd before mee,

William Carpenter, assist.

This deed on the other Side & what is above written is Entered in the pub. Records of ye collony of conecticutt Lib. first folo. 91 & 92, this 29 Aprill, 1679.

P. Jno. Allyn, Secretary.

Rochester, June 28th, 1686.

The Deed and testimonies a foregoing are allowed to bee Recorded in the booke of this Province.

R'd Wharton.

Entered upon Record, June 29th, 1686.
P. Jno. Fones, Record'r.

Know all men by these presents, that I, Capt. william Hudson, of Boston, in New England, Vintner, doe by these for and in consideration of full Sattisfaction in hand given and by mee Received, have bargained & Sould, and doe by these pres'ts Bargaine and Sell unto Richard Smith, of Narragansett, his heires and assigness, one hundred Sixty acres of land, more or less, Sittuated and Lyeing in Narragansett Country, bounded on the north by the land of mr. Amos Richardson, on the South by the land of Rich'd Smith, on the East by the land of maj'or Winslow now in the possession of mr. John Viall, and on the west bounded by the common path or rodewaye, all wch bove s'd land Except twentie and five acres wch is to be layd out at the discretion of Rich'd Smith for Capt. James Oliver, of Boston, I the above s'd Wm. Hudson, from mee, my heires and assigees doe make over and Sell unto the bove s'd Rich'd Smith, his heires and assignes, to have and to hold for ever, wth all rights, titles, privilidges or comons or after divisions or meadows, wch doe, maye or ought to belonge to ye above s'd tract of land, and doe promise the same to defend from any laying claime to any of ye primesses in my name, by my cause or consent or procurem't whatsoever, In Witness of

(60) this my Act, or deed of Sale, I hereunto bind my Selfe, my heires & assignes, and Sett to my hand and Seale in the yeare of o'r Lord God, One Thousand Six hundred Sixty and Seven, the Second day of this instant, March, and in the Nineteenth yeare of the Raigne of o'r Soveraigne Lord Charles the Second of England, Scotland, france & Ireland King.

Wm. Hudson, & a Seale

Signed, Sealed and possession given
   In the presence of us.
   John Cole,
   John Martine,
   John Carr,

   Rochester, June 28th, 1686.
   mr. John Cole, one of the witnesses above, made Oath yt hee Sawe Capt. Wm. Hudson, Seale & deliver ye deed above, on or aboute ye Daye of the date thereof, & that hee Saw John Martyn and John Carr, The other Wittnesses alsoe Subscribe ye Same,

                Sworne before mee R'd Wharton.
This Deed and Testimoney is allowed to bee recorded.
                            R'd Wharton.
Entered upon Record, June 29th, 1686.
P. Jno. Fones, Record'r.

   To all PEOPLE to whom these pres'ts shall Come, Know yee That whereas Coginiquand & Mossip, Indian Sachems, did by their deed beareing date the twentie seventh day of may in the yeare of o'r Lord, one Thousand Six hundred fiftie & nine, pass and Conveye to mr. Randal Holding and to mr. Samuel Gorton, deceased, both of warwick, in Providence plantation, in New England, a tract or Necke of land *Maze to Smith.* in ye Narragansett Country Called then by the name or names of Nanaquakesett, Homogansett, Anocotuckett, Kesicomuck, alias, Shewotuckett wth a little Island Called Sowanoxett alias, Fox Island, and whereas I the said William Maze, of Newport, in Rhoad Island am by virtue of a Gift from my wifes father, the S'd Samuel Gorton, as alsoe by purchase from John Crandall became Interested in, and proprieto'r of part of the premisses, and whereas I the S'd william Maze by my Deede beareing date wth these presents have Sould & Convieyed to william Taylor and Rich'd Wharton, of Boston, Merchants, all my right and interest in the said Island Called Sowanoxett or Fox Island, together wth all my right, title and interest to and in a Necke of land formerly Called Nonoquassett, alias Homogansett, being part of ye said tract Conveyed by the S'd Indian Sachems To ye Said Randall Holden and the Said Samuel Gorton, as by the Said Deed maye more fully appeare, now I the Said william Maze for divers good Causes, and for a valueable Consideration to mee in hand payd by Rich'd Smith, of Narragansett, gentleman doe by these presents grant, Bargaine, Sell, aliene, Enfeaffe and Confirme to ye S'd Rich'd Smith, his heires and assignes, all my right, title, Claime and interest to and in all the remaind'r of the Said tract of Neckes of land Conveyed by and Derrived from the said Indian Sachems, the Said land lyeing to ye Southward or Eastward of the sayd Rich'd Smith's dwelling house in Narragansett, being bounded by the Rhoad or path on the north and northwest, and by the Salt watter on the East, To have and to hold to him the Said Rich'd Smith, his heires & assignes for Ever, all the P' misses not Conveyed as aforesaid to ye Said Taylor and Wharton, I saye my right, title, interest and part therein wth all the imunities, privilidges and Appurtenances in a good, P'fect, absolute and indefeaceable Estate in fee Simple and in as full, free and ample manner, to Stand Seized therein, as I, my Selfe at any tyme did or might by any right whatsoever, And I the Sayd william Maze, doe by these presents Covenant, promise and grant to and wth the Sayd Rich'd Smyth, his heires and assignes, that ye premisses, and every part thereof are, and shall bee free and Clearly acquitted and Discharged from all former and other giftes, grants, Bargaines, Sales, Joyntures, Dowers, titles and incumbrances whatsoever granted, made, covenanted or any waye contracted by mee the Sayd Wm. Maze or any P'son or P'sons claimeing by, from or und'r mee, In Witness whereof, I hereunto have Sett my hand and Seale this twenty third daye of November, Anno Domi Christi One Thousand Six hundred Eighty and One, and in the three and thirtieth yeare of his Majes'ties reigne.

    Willaiam Maze & a seale.

       his ⟨M⟩ marke.

    Sarah ✗ Maze,

     her marke & a Seale.

Sealed and Delivered in the presence
 of Francis Brinley,
   Simon Grover,
   Lott Strange,
   Rob't Hazard,
Rochester, June 28th, 1686.

Francis Brinley, Esq'r, made oath that hee Saw Wm. Maze, Seale and deliver this deed on or aboute ye daye of the date, and Sett to his name as a Wittness thereto.

          R'd Wharton.

Allowed to bee Recorded.

          R'd Wharton.

Entered upon Record, June ye 29th 1686.

      P. Jno Fones, Record'r,

(61) To all People to whome these Pre'nts Shall come, Know yee that whereas, Coginaquand & Mossip, Indian Saichems, did by their deed Beareing date the twentie Seventh day of May, in the yeare of our Lord, One thousand Six hundred fiftie and nine, make over and Conveye to mee Randall *Holden to Smith.* Holden and mr. Samuel Gorton, deceased, both of warwick, in Providence plantation, in New England, a tracte or Necke of land in the Narragansett Counterey called then by the name or names of Nanaquaesett, Homogansett, Anocotuckett, Kesicomucke, alias Shewotuckett wth litle Island called Sowanoxett alias, ffox Island and whereas, I the said Randall Holden, by my deed beareing date with these presents, have Sould and Conveyed to Wm. Taylor and Rich'd Wharton, of Boston, Merchants, all my right and

interest in the said Island called Sowanoxett or Fox Island, together wth all my right, title and interest, to and in a Neck of land formerly called Nonoquassett, alias Homogansett, being part of the said tract conveyed by the said Indian Sachems, to mee the S'd Randall Holden & the Said Samuel Gorton as by the said deed maye more fully Appeare, Now I the said Randall Holden, for divers good causes and for a valuable consideration to mee in hand paid by Richard Smith, of Narragansett, gentleman doe by these presents, grant, Bargaine, Sell, aliene, Enfeaffe and Confirme to the S'd Richard Smith, his heires and assignes all my right, title, claime and interest to and in all ye Remaind'r of the said tract or Necks of land Conveyed by and Derrived from the Said Indian Sachems, the Said land lyeing to ye Southward or Eastward of the said Richard Smiths Dwelling house in Narragansett being bounded by the Rode or path on the north and northwest, and by the salt watter on the East, To have and to hold to him, said Rich'd Smith, his heires and assignes for Ever, All the primesses not Conveyed as above said to ye said Taylor and Wharton, I say my right, title, interest and part therein, wth all the Imunities, privilidges and appurtinances in a good, P'fect absolute & indefeaciable Estate, and in as full, free and ample man'r to Stand Seized therein as I my Selfe at any tyme did or might by any right whatsoever, and I the said Randall Holden, doe, by these presents, Covenant, Promis and grant to and with the S'd Rich'd Smith, his heires and assignes, that ye premisses and Every part thereof are and shal bee free and clearly acquitted and Discharged from all former and other Giftes, Grantes Bargains Sayles, Joyntures, Dowers, Titles and incumbrances whatsoever Granted, made Covenanted or any waye contracted by mee the Said Randall Holden or any P'son or P'sons Claimeing by, from or und'r mee, In witness whereof I here unto have Sett my hand and Seale this twenty Sixth day of Novemb'r, anno Domi Christi, One thousand Six hundred Eighty and One, and in the three and thirtieth yeare of his

Majesties Reigne.

It is to bee understood by all P'sons that Shall Construe, Paraphrase or Expound all or any particular contained in this deed of Sale, that the true intent and meaning is onely One third Part of the whole tract of land mentioned Being the whole claime and interest of the above s'd Randall Holden, as alsoe doth acquit and Discharge no further but to his owne title and interest or proper part, his heires and Executo'rs, Administrato'rs or assignes, there fore Explained before Signeing and Sealeing to avoid mistakes.

Randall Holden & a Seale.

Signed, Sealed and Delivered
    in the presence of
        Samuel Gorton, asist.,
        Thomas Coddington,
        Benjamin Gorton,

I, Francis Holden, wife of the abovesaid Randall Holden doe consent to the above Deed of Sale and for ever quite claime, witness my hand and Sea[le] This 12th day of May, 1682.

the mark of

Francis ⨍ H Holden & a Seale.

Wittness hereunto
    his marke.
        Petter | X/ Welles,

        William Tanner,

Rochester, June 28th, 1686.
This deed is alowed to bee Recorded.

R'd Wharton.

Entered upon record, June 30th, 1686.

Jno. Fones, Record'r.

(**62**) Articles of agreem't made & Considered by and Between Richard Wharton, of Boston, Esq'r, of ye one part and Thomas Mumford, of Rochester, in ye Kings Province, in behalfe of himselfe & Company on ye other Part in manner & forme, following this sixth day of Octob'r, Any'e Dom y'e, one thousand six hundred eighty six, Imprimis, The said Rich'd Wharton doth for his part Covenant, grant and agree to and wth ye s'd Thomas Mumford & Company that he and they shall have & Peaceably Enjoy ye liberty & freedome of the halfe part of ye brooke or streame coming against or by ye land of ye S'd Rich'd Wharton on Boston Neck, which brooke or streame is now knowne or called by ye Name of Mattatuxett, to Sett up a Mill, make a Mill dam and Joyne it to ye land of ye S'd Wharton, there wth ye free use of his ground adjasent to digg stones & earth as is usually Needfull for ye makeing and up houlding of a Mill dam or haveing ye s'd streame as he or they see cause, and for ye stopping or pounding the water upon ye land of ye s'd Wharton, as need shall Require wth free Egress and Regress to & from ye same for and during ye full & whole time & terme that ye Maine fabrick & Principall worke of ye mill Erected by ye S'd Thomas Mumford & Company shall wth out generall Reparation be there Continued, not hereby prohibiting ye s'd Mumford and Company from repairing ye water Wheele or Cogg wheele, Trunnell or or any other thing about ye S'd Mill that requires frequent amendment incident to all mills, All wayes reserveing to him ye S'd Wharton, his heires and assignes, the comon benifitt of ye S'd Brooke or streame no way prejudiciall to ye s'd mill

Agreement Between Rich'd Wharton & Tho. Mumford and Company.

For and in Consideration of all & singular ye Premisses, The s'd Thomas Mumford doth by their Presents in behalfe of himselfe & Company, Covenant & agree wth and doth oblige himselfe to ye S'd Richard Wharton, his heires & assignes to pay or cause to be paid to him or them forthwith the full sum of tenn pounds in currant money or ye value thereof in such other good payment as Major Rich'd Smith,

Capt. Jno. Fones, and other of his Majes'ties Justices of ye Peace, in ye Kings Province, shall Judge, meete & Equivelent, and that it shall & may be lawfull for ye s'd Rich'd Wharton or assignes, at ye time of ye Ruination & uselessness of ye maine worke & fabrick of ye s'd mill as afore s'd to have & enjoy his right and liberty hereby given to ye s'd Mumford & Company, and that he ye s'd Richard Wharton, his heires or assignes, shall at his or their pleasure Turne ye s'd streame or water course againe, In Wittness whereof ye s'd parties have hereunto sett their hands & seales ye day & yeare first above written.

       Richard Wharton

Witness: John Saffin, Thomas Mumford,
     John Fones,
     Lodowick Updick,

Memorandum that both ye parties within mentioned have mutually agreed this Instruement shall be recorded in ye Records of ye Kings Province, wth convenient speed.

Entered upon Record, octob'r 7th, 1686.

       P. Jno. Fones, Record'r.

Know all men, that I, Samuel Cranston, of Newport, sonn and heire unto Major John Cranston, deceased, for and in Consideration of a valueable sume of money in hand received by which I owne my selfe fully contented & sattisfied, do by *Sam'll Cranston to Rich'd Smith. a deed.* these presents make over, bargaine & sell unto Richard Smith of Narragansett, in ye Kings Province, all my right & Title to and in a certaine tract of land scituate lying and being in Narragansett afore s'd, called Nanaquaxett, Kesecomock, Showoatucket, Bounded on ye South by Anocketucket river, on ye North by ye lands of Richard Smith, and on ye East by ye lands now in ye occupation of Thomas Brookes, And on ye West by the road way that goeth to New London, by mr. Samuel Eldredg, his house which lands was Conveyed to my deceased father by mr.

Samuel Gorton & mr. Randall Houlding of warwick, they buying or procureing it from Cojiquant, alias Tasaquanet, Narragansett Sachem, and Rattified by Pissacus Alias Mosip, The Deed beareing date ye 27th day of May, 1659.

(63) and Ratification ye 19th day of September, 1677, I say all my right & Title that was my deceased fathers, I sell & make over unto Richard Smith, his heires, Executo'rs, Administrato'rs and assignes for Ever, and that without incombrance, Joyntures, Dowers or thirds or any thing whatsoever that may impede his right, and do warrant ye same, from me & my heires and claiming by or under my father's right deceased, The said land being now already in Possession of Richard Smith afore s'd, And to this my Act & deed I sett my hand & seale this 11th of aprill, 1685.

Sam'll Cranston,

Mary Jones,

I, mary Jones above Expressed, do consent to the above deed of sale, and do for Ever quit my claime.
Signed, Sealed and Delivered
    in ye presence of
    Francis Brinley,
    Walter Stephens, Ju'r,
Francis Brinley, Esq'r, one of ye wittnesses above, Testifies that he saw Sam'll Cranston and Mary Jones seale and deliver ye Instruem't above as their act & deed on or about the day of ye date thereof, and also saw Walter Stephens, the other Wittness thereof subscribe ye same.

              Sworne before   J. Dudley, P'ent.
Memorandum that ye words which are blotted above are these (viz. Conveyed to my Deceased father, by
    Testis Walter Stephens, Ju'r.

Rochester, Octob'r 7th, 1682.

mr. Walter Stephens appeared before mee the Subscriber, being one of his majes'ties Councill for his Territory & Dominion of New England, and made oath that he saw mr. Sam'll Cranston & mrs. Mary Jones, Signe, Seale & deliver ye within written Instruem't as their act & deed, and that he then subscribed his name as a witness their of.

R'd Wharton.

Entred upon Record, octob'r 11th, 1686.

P. Jno. Fones, Record'r.

To all CHRISTIAN PEOPLE to whome these P'sent deed of Sale shall come, John Vyall, of Swansey, in his Maj'ties Colloney, of New Plimouth, in New England, and Elizabeth, his wife, send greeteing.

KNOW YEE that the Said John Vyall and Elizabeth, his wife, for and in Consideration of the sume of Sixty pounds, *Viall to Smith.* of currant money of New England, to them in hand at & before the Ensealeing and dellivery of these presents by Rich'd Smith of Narragansett, als the Kings Province in New England afore s'd, Gent well and truly paid the receipt, whereof they doe hereby acknowledge and themselves therewith to bee fully Sattisfied and contented, and there of and of every part thereof doe acquit, Exonerate and Discharge the S'd Richard Smith, his heires, Executors and Administrato'rs for ever, by these presents HAVE given, Granted, Bargained, Sold, Aliened, Enfeaffed and Confirmed, and by these presents doe fully, freely, Clearly and absolutely give, grant, Bargaine, Sell, aliene, Enfeaffe and Confirme unto the Said Richard Smith, his heires and assignes for ever, ALL that their own Quarter or fourth part of a certaine farme or tract of land Sittuate, Lyeing and being at a certaine place commonly called and Knowne by the name of Wash Quauge upon Boston neck in s'd Province, which s'd farme containeth by Estimation Six hundred Sixty one acres and an halfe, bee the Same more or less, and is the Southeren purchase made by Maj'r Humph Atherton and Company in the said Province and is now in the tenure and occupation of Joseph Case and John Snooke or their or any one of their assignes, And alsoe all Surplusses, Enlargements, additions by giftes, grantes, Bequestts or otherwise to the S'd one quarter or fourth part of the said southern purchase als belonging together with all houses, Edifices, building, fences, trees, woods, underwoods, Swamps, Meadows, Marshes, Rivers, proffitts, privilidges, Rights, Commodities and appurtenances whatsoever to the Said one quarter or fourth part of the s'd, of the said tract of land or farme bellonging or in any wise appertaineing; To HAVE AND TO HOLD the said one quarter or fourth part of the Said farme or tract of land, with all other the above granted premisses, with their appertenances & every part and parcell thereof, unto the said Richard Smith, his heires and assignes and to the onley proper use, benefitt and behoofe of the s'd Richard Smith, his heires and assignes for ever, and the s'd John Vyall and Elizabeth, his wife, for them selves, their heires, Executo'rs and Administrat'rs doe hereby

(**64**) Covenant, promise and grant to and with the said Richard Smith, his heires and assignes, in manner and form following, (that is to say,) That they the Said John Vyall and Elizabeth, his wife, are the true, Sole and Lawfull owners of all the afore bargained premissess and that they have in Them Selves full power, good right and Lawfull Authoritie to grant, Sell, conveye and assure the same unto the said Richard Smith, his heires and assignes, as a good perfect and absolute Estate of Inheritance in fee Simple, without any Condition, Reversion or Limitation whatsoever, Soe as to Alter change, Defeate or make voyd the Same and that the Said Richard Smith, his heires and assignes Shall and maye by force and vertue of these presents from time to time and at all times, forever, hereafter, Lawfully, peaceably and quietly have, hold, use, occupie, possess and enjoye the above granted premissess with their appurtenances and every part

and parcell thereof free and Clear, and Clearly acquite and
discharged of and from all and all man'r of former and other
giftes, grants, bargaines, Sales, Leases, Mortgages, Jointures, Dowers, Judgem'ts, Executions, Entailes, forfetures and
of and from all other titles, troubles and encombrances whatsoever had made, Committed, done or Suffered to be done by
the Said John Vyall and Elizabeth, his wife, or either of them,
their or either of their heires or assignes, at any time or times
before ye Ensealeing hereof, and further that the S'd John
Vyall and Elizabeth, his wife, their heires, Executo'rs,
Administrato'rs Or Assignes Shall and will from time to time
& Att all times forever, hereafter, warrant and Defend the
above granted premisses with their appurtenances, and every
part and parcell thereof unto the said Richard Smith, his
heires and assignes against all and Every P'son or P'sons
whatsoever, any waies Lawfully Claimeing or demanding the
Same or any part or parcell thereof, by, from or und'r them
the Said John Vyall, Senio'r, and Elizabeth, his wife, or
either of them, their or either of their heires or assignes; in
Witness whereof the S'd John Vyall and Elizabeth his wife,
have hereunto Sett their hands and Seales the twenty fifth
day of May, Anno Domi One thousand Six hundred Eighty
and five anno ye R R Jacobi Secundi Anglia &c. primo.

John Vyall & a (seal) Appending.

      Elizabeth Vyall & a (seal) appending.

In Boston.

 The within written Instruem't was acknowledged by the
within named, John Vyall and Elizabeth his wife, to bee their
act and Deed the 25th of May, 1685.

    before mee Elisha Hutchinson, Assist.

Signed, Sealed and Dellivered in the
presence of us,
John Thomas,
John Hayward, Not. Pub.
Entered upon Record Octo'r 11th, 1686.
P. Jno. Fones, Record'r.

Know all men by these presents, that I, Jonathan Atherton of Dorchester, heire and Administrato'r unto my deceas'd father's Estate, doe by these presents for and in Consideration of full Sattisfaction, for hand given and by mee Received, Bargaine and Sell unto Richard Smith of Narragansett, one parcell of lands in the northerne purchase, Containeing by Estimation one hundred and Sixty acres, more or less, Bounded on the East and Southeast by the lands

(65) of Samuel Dyre, on the north by the lands of Robert Spink, on the west *Jonathan Atherton to Smith* by the lands of william Costing and northwest by the lands late in the possession John Winthrop, Esq., on the South by the lands of John Vyall, all which lands, privilidges, appurtenances and Immunities thereunto bellonging or in any waies appertaining to the Said Lands, I doe alienate, Sell and make over from mee, my heires, Execut'rs & Administrato'rs for ever, unto the above s'd Rich'd Smith, his heires, Executo'rs and Administrat'rs or assignes Forever, and to hold the s'd Lands wth all and Singular, the privilidges and Appurtenances bellonging or in and waies Appertaineing for Ever without any lett, hinderancse, Claime or Molestation by, from or und'r mee whatsoever; In Wittness of all above written, I the s'd Jonathan Atherton have sett my hand & Seale this first day of Aprill, Anno Dom 1673 and in the twenty fifth yeare of his Majes'ties Reigne, Carolus Second of England &c. King.

Jonathan Atherton & a

Signed, Sealed, dellivered and possession
 given in the presence of
John Brigs,
Geo. Codner,
Rich'd Updick,

Know all men by these presents, that I, Rich'd Smith above said, have bargained and Sold, and by these presents doe bargaine and Sell unto francis Brinley, of Newport, the one halfe of the aboves'd Land and privilidges thereunto bellonging, haveing rec'd Sattisfaction for the Same and doe Engage to make, Seale and delliver unto the s'd Francis, his heires or assignes, a firm deed of sale for the Same when required, thereto as wittness my hand in Newport the 10th of august, 1675.

Rochest'r in the Kings Province, July 28th, 1686, John Briggs one of the wittnesses unto this deed of sale, Appeared before mee and did upon oath declare that hee did See Jonathan Atherton Signe, Seale and delliver the Same unto Rich'd Smith as his Reall Act and deed, and alsoe yt hee did See the other two wittnesses mentioned in S'd deed, Viz., Geo. Codner and Rich'd Updick, Attest thereto by Setting to their hands as is Therein wretten.

John Fones,

Roch'r, Oct'r 8, 1686, John Briggs appeared before mee the Subscriber being one of his Majes'ties Councill for his Territory and Dominion of New England, in America, and Declared Opon his form'r Oath, that hee saw mr. Jonathan Atherton, Signe, Seale & Delliver the Instruem't on the other Side, and that hee then Subscribed his name as a Wittness, & Saw Geo. Codner and Rich'd Updick the other wittnesses thereto dated the Sixe.

Rich Wharton.

Entered upon Record Octo. 12, 1686,
Jno. Fones, Record'r.

To all Christian People to whome these presents Shall come, Richard Smith, of Narragansett, in the Kings Province, Sendeth greeting.

Know yee that I, the S'd Richard Smith, for the valuable Consideration of tenn pounds to mee in hand paid, before the Ensealeing and dellivery of these pres'nts, By Francis Brinley, of Newport, in Rhoad Island, have granted, Bargained, *Smith to Brinley.* Aliened, Sold, Enfeaffed and Confirmed and by these presents doe grant, Bargaine, alienate, Sell, En- and Confirme unto the S'd Francis Brinley, his heires and assignes for Ever, One halfe of a certaine parcell of land Bought of Capt. Jonathan Atherton, being one share of the northward purchase in Narragansestt, Containeing by Estimation one hundred

(66) and Sixty Acres more or lesse, Bounded on the East and South East by the lands of Samuel Dyre, on the North by the Lands of Rob't Spink, on the west by the Lands of William Costing, and north west by the lands Late in the possession of John Winthrop, Esq'r, on the South by the lands of John Viall as alsoe the one halfe of the Privilidges, Appurtenances and Immunities thereunto bellonging, or in any wise appurtaineing, To have and to hold the S'd halfe parcell of land and premisses Together with all and Singular, the Appurtenances and privilidges afore Expressed, Unto him the S'd Francis Brinley, his heires and assignes unto the proper use & Behoofe of him the S'd Francis Brinley, his heires and assignes for Ever, And I the S'd Richard Smith, for mee, my heires, Executors and Administrato'rs doe hereby Covenant and promise to and with the S'd Francis Brinley, his heires, Executo'rs, Administrato'rs and assignes that at the time of the Sealeing and dellivering of these Presents, I am Seized of the S'd parcell of Land and premisses herein above granted and Sold in a good and indefeaseable Estate in fee Simple, and have full and Lawfull power and right to Bargaine and Sell the Same

in manner and forme as it is in these presents above Expressed, and I the S'd Richard Smith, the S'd halfe parcell of Land and premisses with all and Singular the Appurtenances above Recited, hereby granted and Sold unto him the S'd Francis Brinley, his heires and assignes against mee, my heires and assignes or any person Claimeing by, from or under mee, will warrant and for Ever defend by these presents, In wittness whereof I have hereunto Sett my hand and Seale the Sixth day of Sept'r, in the Seaven and twentieth yeare of the Reigne of our Soveraigne Lord Charles The Second by the grace of God, of England, Scotland, France and Ireland King; Defend'r of the faith &c Anno qr Domi 1675.

        Richard Smith a   appended.

Sealed and dellivered in the presence of
These words Sendeth greeting & in Narragansett being first interlined.
 Jireh Bull,
   his marke
  James   Sweet,

Elizabeth Burden,
Boston ye 25th Aug'st, 1686.
Rich'd Smith personally Appeareing before mee, under written, one of his Maj'ties Councill in this his Territory and Dominion, acknowledged ye within written
 Instruem't to bee his Act and Deed.
              John Usher.
Entered upon Record Octo'r 12th, 1686.
        P. Jno. Fones, Record'r.

To all persons to whome these presents shall come, Thomas Newton, Marriner, Sendeth greeting, Know yee, yt I the S'd Thomas Newton for and in Consideration of the sume of tenn pounds, New England Money, unto mee in hand paid before the Sealeing and dellivery of these Presents, By Francis Brinley of Newport, the Receipt whereof I doe hereby ac-

Newton to Brinley. knowledge, have granted, Aliened, Bargained, Sold, Enfeaffed and Confirmed, and by these presents for mee, my heires, Executo'rs, and Administrato'rs doe firmely, Clearely and Absolutely, grant, Aliene, Bargaine, Sell and Confirme unto the S'd Francis Brinley, his heires and Assignes for ever, all my right, title, and interest in or unto any Land or Lands or any part or parcell thereof in the Neck comonly called Boston Neck or in any other part of the Narragansett Country, or parts adjacent or which at any time hereafter maye become due unto mee by virtue of my Deceased Grand father, Rich'd Smith, Senio'r, of Narragansett, his last will & testament, as maye more fully appeare, Refferance thereunto being had together with all and Singular, the Liberties, privilidges and advantages to the S'd Land or Lands

(67) Bellonging, to have and to hold the said Land or Lands above by these presents granted, Together wth all and Singular the Premisses thereunto bellonging, unto him the Said Francis Brinley, his heires and assignes for ever, for and to ye onley proper use, and behoofe of him ye S'd Francis Brinley, his heires and assignes for ever, and I the S'd Thomas Newton for mee, my heires, Execut'rs and Administrat'rs doe hereby Covenant and promise to and with the Said Francis Brinley, his heires, Execut'rs, Administrat'rs and assignes for ever that ye Primisses above by these pr'ts of granted, Shall forever, hereafter, bee and remaine in the possession of him the S'd Francis Brinley, his heires and assignes for ever, freely, acquitted, Exonerated and Discharged of and from all manner of former gifts, grants, Bargaines, Salles, Leases and incumbrances, and of and from all other charges, titles and Claimes whatsoever had, made, Suffered or done, or to bee had, made, Suffered or done by mee the S'd Thomas Newton, or by any

other P'son or P'sons whatsoever ,Lawfully Claimeing under mee the S'd Thomas Newton or by any meanes, Title or procurement, And further I the Said Thomas Newton, the Said Land and Lands & all and Singular the primissess above, by these presents granted unto him the S'd francis Brinley, his heires and assignes for Ever, against mee, my heires and assignes, will warrant and for ever defend by these presents, In wittness whereof I have hereto Sett my hand and Seale the 14th day of Decemb'r, 1674.

      Thomas Newton & a

Signed, Sealed & delivered
 in the presence of

    Robert R ✗ Taylor.
      his marke
 Francis Weste.

This deed was Owned by Thomas Newton above S'd to bee his free Act this 20 day of Decemb'r, 1674.
     before mee Rich'd Smith, Com'r.

Rochester, Sept'r 25th, 1686; Then personally Appeared Francis weste, who did declare upon Oath that hee did see Thomas Newton, Signe, Seale and delliver the above written Instruem't unto mr. Francis Brinley, and that Rob't Taylor the other wittness did Attest and Sett his hand as a wittness with him at ye Same time before John Fones, Justice.

 The aforegoing was acknowledged by Francis Weste, upon his former Oath, Rochester 6th, 1686.
      before Rich'd Wharton.
Entered upon Record
 Octo'r 12th, 1686. P. Jno. Fones, Record'r.

 Whereas the Court at Hartford hath granted unto Capt. Jonathan Atherton Lett'rs of Administration of the Estate of Maj'r Humphrey Atherton Deceased, Lyeing and being in ye Narragansett Country &c., and hee the S'd Jonathan Atherton by virtue of his above Said Power hath Bargained and Sold unto mr. Rich'd Smith of Narragansett, two tracts of Land therein, one Containeing Seven hundred acres lyeing and being in the Neck Called Boston Necke and adjourning to Pettequamscutt Harbor, the other in the Northward Purchase being a Whole Share thereof wth all privilidges Thereto Bellonging.

<small>*Confirmation Atherton's to Smith.*</small>

Now Know all men by these Presents, that wee, Hope Atherton, Consider Atherton, Watching Atherton and Joseph Wicks for our Selves, Heires, Execut'rs, Administrat'rs and assignes doe hereby owne, acknowledge, Rattifie and Confirme the Sale of the Said Lands &c., unto Richard Smith above S'd, his heires, Execut'rs and assignes, to have & to hold the S'd Land and premisses to him the Said Rich'd Smith, his heires and assignes for ever, and doe hereby acknowledge to have received of Said Richard Smith, forty pounds Currant money of new England, Before the Sealeing and Dellivery hereof by the Appointm't of S'd Jonathan Atherton being in part of paym't of our rights and Shares therein, the whole being one hundred and Seventy pounds as maye more fully appear by the deeds thereof, Refferance being thereunto had, In Wittness whereof wee have hereunto putt o'r hands & Seales the 19th of June, 1674.

Hope Atherton & a

Consider Atherton & a

Watching Atherton & a

John Wicks & a

Signed, Sealed and delivered in the
presence of John Green,
        Geo. Wightman,
        Francis Brinley,

(**68**) Rochest'r in the Kings Province, July 26th, 1686. Francis Brinley one of the wittnesses of the within written deed, appeared before mee and did declare upon Oath, yt hee did see hope Atherton, Consider Atherton, Watching Atherton and Joseph Weekes Signe, Seale and delliver ye Same unto mr. Richard Smith as their Reall act and deed.
                                      John Fones.

Rochest'r, Octo'r 5th, 1686.

    mr. Francis Brinley and Geo. Wightman Appeared before mee, the Subscriber, Being one of his Maj'ties Councill for this his Territory and Dominion of New England in America, and made Oath yt they Saw Hope Atherton, Consider Atherton, Watching Atherton and Joseph Weeks Signe, Seale and Deliver the within written Instruem't as their Act and Deed on or aboute the daye of the date thereof, and yt they the Deponenants then Subscribed their names as wittnesses thereof.

    Sworne Octo. 5th, 1686.
                      before   Rich'd Wharton.

Entered upon Record, Octob'r 12th, 1686.
                      P. Jno. Fones, Record'r.

    To all people to whom these Pres'ts shall come, I Jonathan Atherton of Dorchester, in the Massachusetts Collony in New England, Son and heir to Humphrey Atherton of the S'd Dorchester deceas'd, and Administrato'r to ye Estate of the S'd Humphrey Atherton, Lyeing in the Narragansett Country in the Collony of Rhoad Island and Providence Plantations &c., Send greeteing.

Jonathan Atherton to Richard Smith.

    Know yee that I, the Said Jonathan Atherton for and in Consideration of the Sum of fifty Pounds money in England

and one hundred Pounds in New England money unto mee in hand paid by Rich'd Smith of Narragansett, In the Kings Province, the receipt whereof I doe hereby acknowledge & therewirh doe owne my Selfe to bee fully Sattisfied, contented, and paid have, granted, Aliened, Enfeaffed, Bargained and Sold, and by these Presents for mee, my heires, Execut'rs and Administrato'rs, doe fully and Clearly and Absolutely grant, Alien, Enfeaffe, Bargaine, Sell and Confirme unto the S'd Rich'd Smith, his heires and assignes for ever a Certaine parcell of Land Lieing Southermost in the greate Necke commonly called Boston Necke in the Narragansett Country, in the Kings Province, and is adjourning to the Harbour commonly called Pettaquamscutt Harbo'r, being a whole share of that Purchase, and is aboute Seven hundred Acres or land more or less being now in the possession of Geo. Craft my tennent, together wth all & Singular, the Houses, out houses Barnes, Stables, Edefices, gardens, Orchards, fences, Commons, Liberties, waies, high waies, priviildges and Appurtainances on, on the S'd Land being or to the Same or to any part or parcell thereof bellonging or in any wise appurtaineing to have and to hold the S'd Land together with all and Singular the Premisses above by these presents granted unto him the Said Rich'd Smith, his heires and assignes to the proper use and behoofe of him the S'd Rich'd Smith, his heires and assignes for ever, and I s'd Jonathan Atherton the said Land together wth all and Singular, the premisse above by these presents granted unto him the S'd Richard Smith, his heires and assignes against mee, my heires and assignes will warrant and for ever defend by these presents and I the S'd Jonathan Atherton for mee, my heires, Execu to'rs and Administrato'rs doe hereby Covenant and promis to and with S'd Richard Smith, his heires, Executo'rs, Administrato'rs and assignes, That I am Seized of the Said land and every part and parcell thereof

together with all and

Singular, the premisses above by these presents granted in a good and indefeaseable Estate of fee Simple and have full power to grant, Alien, bargaine, and Sell the Same to him the S'd Richard Smith, his heires and assignes, in manner and forme above in these presents Expressed and that the Said Land and every part and parcell thereof Shall for ever hereafter bee and remaine unto the Said Richard Smith, his heires and assignes, fully and Clearly Exonerate, acquitted and Discharged of and from all and all manner of former bargaines, giftes, grants, leases, demands, Jointures, Dowers and all other charges and incombrances whatsoever had made, ordered, or to bee made, had or done by mee the S'd Jonathan Atherton or by any other person or Persons by my means, title or Procurem't in wittnes whereof, I the S'd Jonathan Atherton have hereunto Sett my hand and Seale the three and twentieth day of July, in the five and twentieth yeare of the Reigne of our Soverigne Lord Charles The Second, by the grace of God, King of England, Scotland, france and Ireland &c., Annoqr'e Domi 1673.

      Jonathan Atherton & a

Signed, Sealed and Delivered
 On the presence of us,
  Francis Brinley,
  Richard Updick,
  Edmund Oliver,
  Elizabeth P. Garratt.

Appeared before mee the 24th of July 1673 Jonathan Atherton above mentioned and owned the above written Instruem't to bee his Act and deed.
      william Coddington, Dep't Gov'r.

The above written deed and acknowledgm't was entered and Recorded in the publicke Records of his Maj'ties Collony of Rhoad Island and Providence Plantations, in the

37th page of the booke of land.

Evidences this 20th day of aug'st, 1673, as attest.
John Sanford, Record'r.

Entered upon Record this 12th Octob'r, 1686.
P. Jno. Fones, Record'r.

To all people to whome these Presents shall come, I Richard Smith, of Narragansett in the Kings Province, Send greeteing.

Know yee that I the Richard Smith, for and in consideration of the sum of fifety pounds Lawfull money in England, and one hundred pounds in New England money, *Smith to Brinley.* unto mee in hand paid by francis Brinley, of Newport in Rhoad Island, the receipt whereof I doe hereby acknowledge and therewith doe owne my Selfe to bee fully Sattisfied, contented and paid, have granted, Bargained, aliened, Sold, Enfeaffed and Confirmed, and by these Presents, for mee, my heires, Executo'rs & Administrat'rs doe fully, clearly and Absolutely grant, Bargaine, alien, Sell, Enfeaffe and confirme unto ye Said francis Brinley, his heires & assignes for ever, a certaine parcell or tract of Land lyeing Southermost in the greate neck comonly called Boston Necke, in the Narragansett Country, in the Kings Province, and is adjourning to the Harbour comonly called Pettequamocutt harbour, being a whole share of that Purchase, & is aboute seven hundred acres of land more or lesse, being now in Possession of George Craft tenant, thereon together with all and Singular, the houses, Outhouses, Barnes, Stables, Edifices, gardens, Orchards, fences, Commons, liberties, wayes, Highwayes, Privilidges and Appurtenances on the S'd land being or to the same or to any part or parcell thereof Bellonging or in any wise appurtaineing, to have and to hold the Said Land together with all and Singular, the premisses above by these presents granted

(70) unto him the said francis Brinley, his heires and assignes for ever, and I the said Richard Smith, the Said Land together with all and Singular, the premisses above by these Presents granted unto him the Said francis Brinley, his heires and assignes, aga'st mee, my heires & assignes, will warrant and forever Defend by these presents, and I the Said Richard Smith, for mee, my heires, Execut'rs and Administrato'rs doe hereby Covenante and promise to and with the said francis Brinley, his heires, Execut'rs, Administrat'rs and assignes, yt I am Seized of ye Said land and every part and parcell thereof together with all and Singular, the premisses above by these presents granted in a good and indefeaseable Estate of fee Simple, and have full power to grant, aliene, Bargaine and Sell the Same to him the Said francis Brinley, his heires and assignes, in maner and forme above in these presents Expressed, and that the Said land and every part and parcell thereof Shall forever, here after, bee and remaine unto ye Said francis Brinley, his heires and assignes fully and clearly exonerated, acquitted and discharged of and from all and all maner of former Bargaines, gifts, grantes, leases, demands, Jointures, Dowers and all other Charges and incumbrances whatsoever had, made or done or to bee made, had or done by mee the said Richard Smith, or by any other person or persons by my meanes, title or procurement; in Wittness whereof, I the Said Richard Smith, have hereunto sett my hand and Seale the fifteenth day of february, in the Six and Twentieth yeare of the raigne of o'r Soveraigne Lord Charles the Second King of England, Scotland, france and Ireland &c., Annoq'e Domi 1673.

Richard Smith,

Signed, Sealed and Delivered
   In the presence of
      Ann Coddington,
      John Coddington,

This deed of Sale above mentioned was Signed, Sealed and dellivered before mee.

William Coddington, Deputy.

The above written deed of Sale with the Attestation thereunto is Entered on Record in the 198 page of the booke of Land Evidences No. 3 bellonging to the towne of Newport.

P. Weston Clarke, Towne Clerke.

Entered upon Record, Octob'r 22th, 1686.

P. Jno. Fones, Record'r.

These Presents wittnesseth that wee whose names are under written, being Concerned in our deceased fathers, Maj'r Humphrey Atherton's Estate.

Wee doe by these Presents Ratifie and confirme a deed of *Confirmation of Atherton to Smith.* Land Sold by our Brother Jonathan Atherton of Seven hundred Acres, Situated in Boston Necke neare Wachquage, In Narragansett, as wittness our hand this 12th day Novemb'r, 1674.

Wittness hereunto	Timothy Mather,
Lodawick Updick,	James Trowbridge.
	Patience Atherton.

Rochester in the Kings Province, July 26, 1686, Lodowick Updick, Wittness unto ye above written Instruem't personally Appeared before mee, and did upon Oath declare yt hee did See Timothy Mather, James Trowbridge and Patience Atherton, Signe and Acknowledge the S'd Instruem't.

John Fones.

Rochester, Octob'r 6th. 1686, Maj'r Rich'd Smith and Lodowick Updick personally appeared before mee the Subscriber, and made Oath yt they Saw mr. Timothy Mather, Signed the above written Instruem't & heard James Trowbridge and Patience Atherton declare their consent thereto.

Rich'd Wharton.

Entred upon Record, Octob'r 22, 1686.

P. Jno. Fones, Record'r.

(71) To all People to whome these presents shall come, greeting, Know yee yt I, Capt. Jonathan Atherton, of Dorchester, being Administrat'r to ye Estate of Maj'r Humphrey Atherton, Lyeing and beinge in the Narragansett country, in the Colony of Conecticutt, for a Valuable Consideration in hand paid unto mee by Francis Brinly, of Newport, in Rhoad Island, the receipt Whereof I hereby acknowledge & am therewith fully Sattisfied, contented and paid, have granted, Bargained, aliened, Sold, enfeaffed and confirmed, and by these presents doe grante, Bargaine, aliene, Sell, Enfeaffe and confirme unto ye Said Francis Brinly and his heires, Executo'rs, Administrat'rs and assignes, all my right, title, interest, Privilidge & Propriety, in any part or parts, parcell or parcells of land purchased or given to my father, Maj'r Humphrey Atherton, in the S'd Narragansett Countrey, bee it either in the Lands called ye Mortgage Lands or in the Purchase of Point Judith Neck or Elsewhere in the Said Narragansett Countrey, which now maye or hereafter shall Become due unto mee, ye S d Jonathan Atherton, by Virtue of my Lett'rs of Administration above mentioned or as being ye Eldest Son of Maj'r Humphrey Atherton above said, or by any other waies or meanes whatsoever (Except what lands are already Sold by mee to mr. Rich'd Smith of above Said Narragansett,) together wth all Privilidges & Immunities, thereunto bellonging or in any wise appurtaineing or hereafter shall bee, To have and to hold the Said land or lands and Privilidges thereunto bellonging To the Said Francis Brinley, and his heires, Execut'rs, Administrat'rs & assignes, to the Onley proper use, and behoofe of him ye Said Francis Brinley, his heires & assignes for Ever, and I the S'd Jonathan Atherton, for my heires, Execut'rs, Administrat'rs and Assignes doe Covenant & Promise & agree to and with ye Said Francis Brinley, That I am Rightfully Seized of the

Jonathan Atherton to Francis Brinly.

Said lands and have full power & Lawfull Authority to Sell and Dispose ye Same and the Said Francis Brinley and his heires &c., in the Possession of the said lands against any P'son or P'sons Lawfully claiming anything by, from or under mee or mein Will for ever warrant and Defend by These presents, and further doe ingage my Selfe, heires & assignes to give Such Lyall observance as the Said Francis Brinley, or his heires, Shall require of mee; In Wittness Whereof I have hereunto Sett my hand and Seale in Boston, the 20th of November, 1674.

      Jonathan Atherton & a

memo. the words in the 6th line, Executo'rs, Administrat'rs and assignes were Enterlined before ye Sealeing & dellivery hereof.

Signed, Sealed and dellivered in
 The presence of us,
  Lott Strange,
  John Williams.

John Williams, one of the Wittnesses to the deed, Appeared before mee & tooke his Oath yt hee was present When Jonathan Atherton Signed, Sealed & dellivered this Instruem't to mr. Francis Brinley, as his Act and deed, and Alsoe did see Lott Strange Signe the Same, as a Wittness wth himselfe taken upon Oath ye 1st day of July, 1686, before mee

      John Coggeshall, Dep'y Gov'r.

John Williams alsoe testyfied the same before mee Aug't ye 9th, 1686.

      Walter Clarke, Gov'r.

To Capt. Jno. Fones, in Roch'r Kings Province, the 13th Aug't, 1686, Mr. Record'r the above Written deed & proofs thereof ye wittnesses being in another Governm't was directed by my Selfe to bee made in Such forme as it now is, and is hereby allowed to pass into the Records of the Kings Province.

P. mee J. Dudley, Pres't.

Entered upon Record, Octob'r 22, 1686.

P. Jno. Fones, Record'r.

(**72**) To all people to whom these presents Shall come I, Richard Updick, of Narragansett, In Kings Province, Cooper Send Greeting. Know yee, that I the Said Richard Updick, for and in Consideration of ye Sum of tenn Pounds, New England money, to mee in hand paid before ye Enseale- *Richard Updick to Francis Brinly* inge & dellivery of these Presents, by Francis Brinley, of Newport in Rhoad Island, the receipt whereof I doe hereby acknowledge, and of ye Same and every part therof, doe hereby fully acquitt, Release, and Discharge ye Said Francis Brinley, his heires and assignes, have granted, Bargained, aliened, Sold, Enfeaffed and Confirmed, and by these presents doe fully, freely and absolutely grant, Bargaine, Alien, Sell, Enfeaffe and confirmed unto ye Said Francis Brinley, his heires & assignes for ever, all my right, title and interest in the Lands In Narragansett Countrey lyeing to ye Southward of my Uncle Smith's tradeing house, which was left mee as a Legacie in ye Last will and testament of my grand father, Richard Smith Deceased, as Rellation being had to ye Said will maye more amply appeare, as alsoe all and Singular, the Rights, Privilidges and Appurtainances to yee Same Bellonging or in any wise appurtaineing, To have and to hold the Said lands and Premisses, Soe Bequeathed unto mee as afore said, together wth all and Singular, the rights, Privilidges & Appurtenances afore recited unto him ye Said Francis Brinley, his heires and assignes, unto ye Proper use, behoofe & benefitt of him ye Said Francis Brinley, his heires and assignes for ever, and I the Said Rich'd Updick, for mee, my heires, Execut'rs and administrat'rs doe hereby Covenant and Promise to and with the Said Francis Brinley, his heires, Execut'rs, administrat'rs and assignes, That att ye time of the Sealeing and dellivery of these Presents, I am Seized of the Said Lands and premisses herein above granted and Sold in a good and Indefeasable Estate in fee Simple, and have full and Lawfull power and right to Bargaine and Sell ye same in maner and forme as it is in these Presents above Expressed, and I the Said Richard Updick, the Said Lands & Primisses with all and Singular, the Appurtainances above Expressed, hereby granted and Sold unto him the Said Francis Brinley, his heires & assignes, against mee, my heires and assignes, or any P'son claimeing by, from or under mee, will warrant and for Ever defend by the Presents; In Wittness whereof I have hereunto Sett my hand and Seale the twentie Sixth day of Septemb'r, In the Seven and twentieth yeare of the reigne of o'r Soveraigne Lord Charles the Second, by the grace of god, King of England, Scotland, france and Ireland, defender of the faith &c. annoqr Domi 1675.

Richard Updick & a

Signed, Sealed and Delivered
  in the presence of
    John Fones,
    Elizabeth Burden,
    Josiah Sylvester.

Rochest'r, in the Kings Province, July 26th, 1686, John Fones, one of the Wittnesses to ye within written deed of Sale, appeared before mee and did declare Upon Oath yt hee did See Rich'd Updick, Signe Seale and Delliver ye same as his reall act & deed.

Rich'd Smith.

(73) Boston, Septemb'r 28th, 1686, mrs. Elizabeth Burden, appeared before mee, under written, one of his Maj'ties Councill of his Territory and Dominion of New England, and made Oath yt She saw Richard Updick Signe,

Seale and Delliver the within written Instruem't as his Act and Deed, and yt She Sett her hand to it as a Wittness.
Waite Winthrop.

Rochest'r, in the Kings Province, Octob'r 13th, 1686, John Fones above mentioned did in open Court averre to what hee had upon oath declared before mee.
J. Winthrop.

Entered upon Record, Octo'r 22th, 1686.
P. Jno Fones, Record'r,

Whereas o'r Brother Jonathan Atherton being Administrato'r to ye Estate of Maj'r Humphrey Atherton deceased, appointed by the Collony of Conecticut, Lyeing & being in the said Jurrisdiction, Viz., in ye Narragansett Country comonly Called ye Kings Province, and hee ye s'd Capt. Atherton haveing Sold unto mr. Rich'd Smith of said Narragansett, a tract of land lyeing in Boston Neck in ye Said Narragansett, being aboute Seven hundred Acres of Land Adjourning to ye Harbour att Pittaquamscutt, wth all privilidges and Emmunities thereunto Bellonging, as maye appeare by a deed thereof, and unto ye Said Rich'd Smith, Now Know all men by these presents that wee under written being Sons-in-law to ye above said Maj'r Humphrey Atherton, and being thereby Interrested and concerned in the Estate above mentioned, doe hereby Rattifie, allowe and Confirme ye Said Deed of Sale to ye Said Rich'd Smith, and approve thereof, and further doe hereby Surrender up all our right, Interests and Privilidges in ye Said Land or Lands accordinge to the deed thereof made to ye Said Rich'd Smith Without Cover or deceite; In Witness Whereof wee have hereunto Sett our hand & Seales in Boston, the 10th of August, 1674, And further whereas Capt. Jonathan Atherton hath further Sold unto mr. Rich Smith above said a tract of Land being a whole Share Lyeing in Aquidnesett, Wee under written doe hereby Rattifie and Confirme the Sale of the Said tract of

Confirmation of Atherton to Smith.

Land as Wittness our hands ye day and yeare above written.

      Obadiah Swift & a   seale.

      Thomas Bird & a   seale.

      John Clarke & a   seale.

Test
John Freeke,
Waite Winthrop,
Francis Brinley.

Waite Winthrop second witness to this writeing, appeared the 10th X'ber, 1675, & made Oath hee put his name as a Wittness thereto & See it signed by the hands & Seales of ye 3 Subscribers.

This done before mee,   In Boston, N. E.
           Jno. Leverett, Gov'r.

Roch'r, in ye Kings Province, July ye 26th, 1686, Francis Brinley, one of ye Wittnesses of ye within written deed, appeared before mee & did declare upon Oath yt hee did See Obadiah Swift, Thomas Bird and John Clarke, Signe, Seale & delliver ye within written Instruem't unto Rich'd Smith within mentioned as their Reall Act & deed.
             John Fones.

Francis Brinley appeareing before mee, One of his Maj'ties Councill for his Territory and Dominion of New England, this 13th of Octo'r, 1686, testifyed upon Oath yt hee Saw Obadiah Swift, Thomas Bird and John Clarke, Signe, Seale & delliver ye within Instruem't as their act and Deed unto mr. Rich'd Smith within mentioned.
             J. Winthrop.

Entered upon Record, Octob'r 22th, 1686.
P. Jno. Fones, Record'r.

(**74**) Know all men by these presents that I, Richard Smith, of Wickford, In Narragansett doe make over, Bargaine and Sell unto John fones of Quenaniquatt, all my Right, *Smith to Fones.* title and interest to and in a Share of Land I lately bought betweene mr. Francis Brinley and my Selfe, of Capt. Jonathan Atherton, the whole containing One Hundred and fifty acres more or lesse, it being Sittuated and Lyeing in the Northward purchase made by Maj'r Atherton and Company in Narragansett alias Acquidnessett, Bounded on the East and South East entirely by the Lands of Samuel Dyre and John Viall, of Boston, his land in Narragansett one parte of which Samuel Pratt now dwelleth, the halfe of which S'd hundred & fifty acres together With all my Share of all rights and privilidges thereto Bellonging, now or hereafter maye bee appurtaineing by reason of ye Said Purchase, I doe as above make Over, Bargaine and Sell from mee, my heires, Execut'rs, Administrat'rs & assignes, firmely by these presents unto ye above Said John fones, his heires, Executo'rs, administrat'rs and assignes to have and to hold ye Same for ever, without Lett or hindrance from mee or by my means, Cause or Consent, I acknowiedge by these presents to have received full Sattisfaction in hand, in Consideration of the Said Premisses; In wittness of all above I Sett my hand and Seale this 27th daye of January, and in the twentie fourth yeare of his Maj'ties Raigne, Carolus Secondus Angilia &c. Anno Domini 1673-74.

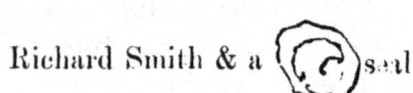

Richard Smith & a seal

Signed, Sealed and Dellivered in the
Presence of Jonathan Atherton,
   Rich'd Updick,
    his marke
  Petter   Welles,

Rochester. June 25th, 1686.

The above written deed was acknowledged by Maj'r Rich'd Smith, before mee ye Subscriber being one of his Maj'ties Councill for his Maj'ties Territory & Dominion of N. England.
        Rich'd Wharton.

Entered upon Record, Octo'r 25th, 1686.
       P. Jno. Fones Record'r.

To all people to whome this present writeing Shall come, John Winthrop Esquire, Govern'r of ye Collony of Connecticutt, in New England, Send greeting. Know yee that I ye Said John Winthrop, for & in Consideration of a valuable Sum in hand paid by Richard Dummer of Newberry, in ye Massachusetts Collony of New England, Gent as for divers other good causes and Considerations, mee ye Said John Winthrop, thereunto moveing, have given, granted, Bargained, Sold, Enfeaffed and confirmed, and by these Presents doe give, grant, Bargaine, Sell, Enfeaffe & Confirme unto ye S'd Rich'd Dummer, his heires and assignes, all my right, title & interest in all yt parcell of land lyeing and being in the Narragansett Country, Containing one hundred and forty and forty [sic] acres, be there more or Less with all ye Rights, privilidges and Appurtenances to ye Same bellonging, Bounded

Winthrop to Dummer.

(75)   According to a platt thereof wth other Lands taken P. mr. Hutchinson, if Rightly taken to have and to hold the afore granted premisses, and all and

every part thereof wth all the rights, privilidges and Appurtinances thereof and thereunto Bellonging as afore Said unto ye Said Richard Dummer, his heires and assignes to ye onley proper use & Behoofe of ye Said Richard Dummer, his heires and assignes for ever in Such large & ample Sort, manner & forme as I the S'd John Winthrop maye grant, Convey and assure ye Same, and that I doe hereby Covenant, for mee, and my heires, yt the afore granted premisses wth all ye rights, Privilidges and Appurtenances thereof as afore said unto he Said Rich'd Dummer, his heires and assignes against mee & my heires, or any claimeing by, from or und'r mee, I shall and will warrant and for ever defend by these presents; In wittness whereof I have hereunto putt my hand and Seale the fourth day of November, in ye yeare of our Lord One thousand Six hundred Sixty nine Annoq'e Regni Regis Caroli Secundi &c., &c.

Postscript. Bettweene ye parties to these presents, It is concluded & Agreed that the Land about granted is bounded wth ye high waye or comon Land, we for, by and with the Land of Amos Richardson Southerly.

John Winthrop & a seale.

This within written deed was Signed, Sealed and Dellivered and ye Postscript wrote and agreed upon, and these words (is Bounded wth ye High) In this Postscript interlined before Sealeing in Presence of Henry Gidley.

Ita attest P. Robert Howard, Not. Publ., Massachusetss Collonie, Nova Anglia.

Entered & Recorded in ye third page of ye 4th booke of ye Not. Publick, his Records of ye Massachusetts Collonie of New England the 13th of Novemb'r, 1669.

P. Robert Howard.

not. Public Collina, Predict.

Entered upon Record, octob'r 25th, 1686.

P. Jno. Fones Record'r.

To all people to whom these presents Shall come, greeting; Know yee, That I Richard Dummer, of Newberry, in the county of Essex, in N. England for severall and good considerations, my Selfe there unto moveing have given, granted, *Dummer to Dummer.* Enfeaffed and Confirmed, and by these presents doe fully, freely, clearly and absolutely give, grant, Enfeaffe and confirm unto my Beloved Son, Jeremiah Dummer, his heires & assignes for Ever, all my right, title and interest in One hundred and forty acres of Land Lyeing at ye Narragansett Country, Which I bought of ye Hon'd Gov'r Winthrop, and Accordingly confirmed to my Selfe by the Said Gov'r by this Instruem't Expressed on ye other Side of this Schdule, to have and to hold ye above granted and Bargained premisses accordinge to ye full Extent of ye afores'd, grant thereof to my Selfe wth all ye Privilidges and Appurtenances to the Same Appurtaineing, or in any wise bellonging to him the Said Jeremiah Dummer, his heires and assignes for Ever to his and their onley Proper use and behoofe, and I the Said, Richard Dummer for my

(76) heires and administrato'rs doe Covenant, Promise and grant to and with The Said Jeremiah, his heires and assignes by these Presents, that hee ye Said Jeremiah, his heires and assignes Shall and may at all times, and from time to time for Ever, hereafter, quietly and peaceably have, hold, Occupy, possess and Enjoye ye Same without ye Lawfull Lett, hindrance, Eviction, Expulsion, Suite or Deniall of mee ye Said Rich'd, my heires, Executo'rs, Administrat'rs or assignes, or any of them or if any other P'son or P'sons whatsoever from, by or und'r mee or by my means or procurem't; In Wittness whereof I the Said, Richard Dummer have afixed my hand & Seale hereunto this Seventh day of July, Anno Domni One thousand Six hundred Seventy & foure.

       Richard Dummer & a   seale.

Signed, Sealed & Dellivered in the
    Presence of us,
      Samuel Bradtebourne.
      Rich'd Dummer, Junio'r.

Rich'd Dummer Acknowledged this writeing to bee his Act & Deed, before mee   Daniel Dennison.
                                              July 9th, 1674.

Entered upon Record Octob'r 25th, 1686.
                P. Jno. Fones, Record'r.

Dummer to Fones. To all people to whom these Presents Shall come, Jeremiah Dummer, of Boston In the Massachusetts Collony of New England, Goldsmith, Sendeth greeting. Know yee that I the Said Jeremiah Dummer, for and in Consideration of ye Sum of forty pounds currant money of New England, to and in hand before the Ensealeing and Dillivery of these Presents well and truely paid by Capt. John Fones, of James towne, alis Cononicott, within the Collony of Rhoad Island in New England afore S'd, the receipt whereof to full content and Sattisfaction, I doe hereby Acknowledge to have given, granted, Bargained, Sold, Enfeaffed and Confirmed, and by these presents doe fully and absolutely give, grant, Bargaine, Sell, enfeaffe and Confirme unto the Said Capt. John fones, his heires and assignes, all my right, title and interest in all that parcell of land lyeing and being in ye Narragansett Country in New England, containeing one hundred and forty acres, bee there more or Less bounded wth ye high way or comon Land westerly, and wth the Land of Amos Richerdson Southerly, wth all rights, privilidges & Appurtainances to ye Same Bellonging, Bounded accordinge to a Platt thereof wth other Lands taken P. mr. Hutchinson, if rightly taken to have and to hold ye afore bargained premisses, and all and every part thereof wth all ye rights, privilidges and Appurtainances thereof and thereunto bellongng formerly purchased by my father, mr. Rich'd Dummer of yᵉ Honorable John Winthrop, Esq'r, Sometime Gov'r of ye Colloneny of Connecticott, & by him Assigned Over unto mee, unto him the Said John fones, his heires and assignes (77) to ye onley proper use and Behoofe of ye Said John fones, his heires and assignes for Ever in Such large and ample Sorte, manner and forme as I the the Said Jeremiah Dummer, maye grant, Convey and assure the Same, and yt I doe hereby Covenant for mee and my heires, yt ye afore granted Primisses wth all ye right, privilidges and Appurtainances thereof, as aforesaid unto ye Said John Fones, his heires and assignes, against mee and my heires or any claimeing by, from or under mee, I shall and will warrant and for Ever defend By these presents, and I doe hereby impow'r my trusty friend, mr. Rich'd Smith, of Narragansett, my Lawfull Attorney for mee and in my name to delliver full possession, And Seizure of ye within Bargained Premisses unto ye Said John Fones; In Wittness whereof, I have hereunto putt my hand and Seale this Eight day of Novemb'r, Anno Domini One thousand Six hundred and Eighty, and in the thirtieth [sic] Second yeare of ye raigne of our Soveraigne Lord King Charles the Second over England &c.

Jere'h Dummer & a seale.

Signed, Sealed & De'd in the presence of us, after interlineing ye words (In New England afore s'd) betweene the 5th and 6th lines, and writeing ye word New England in ye margin.
Rich'd Smith,
Jireth Bull.

I Annah Dummer, wife of ye above named Jeremiah Dummer, doe freely consent unto ye Sale of ye above bargained premisses, and Relinquish all Dow'r or right of thirds therein wittness my hand and Seale ye 8 Novemb'r, 1680,

Anna Dummer & a (seal) seale.

This Instruem't above written was acknowledged by Jeremiah Dummer and Anna his wife, to bee ye Act & deed this 13th Novemb'r, 1680.

Edward Tyng, assist.

Entered upon Record Octo'r 26th, 1686.
P. Jno. Fones, Record'r.

To all christian People to whom this present deed of Sale Shall come, Joshuah Hews, of Boston in the Collony of the Massachusetts in New England, Cordwainer, and Hannah his wife Send greeting: Know yee yt ye Said Joshuah Hews and Hannah his wife, for and in Consideration of the sum of *Hews to Fones* twentie pounds, & of Lawfull money of New England, to y'm in hand at or before the ensealeing & dellivery of these presents by Capt. John Fones of James Towne, alis Connonacutt, in ye Collony of Rhoad Island and Providence plantations, In New England afore S'd, well and truely paid, the receipt whereof they doe hereby Acknowledge, and Themselves therewith fully Sattisfied and contented, and, thereof, & of every part thereof doe acquitt, Exonerate and Discharge the Said John Fones, his heires, Execut'rs, administrato'rs and assignes, and every of them for ever, by these presents have given, granted, Bargained, Sold, aliened, Enfeafed and confirmed, and by these presents doe fully, Clearly and Absolutely give, grant, Bargaine, Sell, alien, Enfeaffe & confirme unto the S'd John Fones, his heires and assignes for ever, All yt their tract or P'sell of land Sittuate, Lyeing and being In ye Narragansett Country, In New

(78) England afore s'd, neere unto ye now Dwelling house of mr. Richard Smith containing by Estimation One hundred & fifty acres, bee ye Same more or Less, being butted

and bounded westerly by the Country Road yt leads from the S'd Smith's towards Stonning towne, Northwardly by the lands of ye Late John Reynolds deceas'd, Easterly by the Land of Robert Spink, and Southerly by the highway, which S'd Land did formerly bellonge to their father, Josuah Hews deceased, together wth all woods, underwoods, trees, Swamps, watters, wattercourses, proffiitts, Privilidges, Rights, commodities, hereditaments and Appurtainances whatsoever to ye Said tract or P'cell of land bellonging or in any wise Appurtaineing, To have & to hold The Said tract or P'cell of Land, Butted and bounded as a fores'd wth all other The above granted premisses unto ye Said John Fones, his heires & assignes, and to ye onley proper use, benefitt and behoofe of ye Said John Fones, his heires and assignes for ever, and ye S'd Joshuah Hews and Hannah his wife, for them Selves, their heires, Executo'rs & Administrat'rs doe hereby covenant, Promise and grant to and wth ye S'd John Fones, his heires and assignes, that at ye time of the Ensealeing hereof they are ye true, Sole and lawfull Owners of all ye afore Bargained primesses and are lawfully Seized of and in the Same and every part thereof in their owne proper right, and that ye Said Joshuah Hews and Hannah his wife, have in them Selves full pow'r, good Right and lawfull Authoritie to grant, Sell, convey and assure ye Same unto the S'd John Fones, his heires and assignes as a good, P'fect and absolute Estate of inheritance in fee Simple, without any man'r of Condition Reversion or Limittation whatsoever, Soe as to alter, change, or make voy'd ye Same, and that ye Said John Fones, his heires and assignes Shall and may from time to time and att all times for ever, hereafter, lawfully, peaceably and quietly have, hold, use, Occupie, Possess and enjoye the above granted premisses wth their Appurtainances free and cleere of and from all & and [sic] all man'r of former and other gifts, grantes, bargaines, Sales, Leases, mortgages, Joyntures, Dowers, Judgments, Executions, Entailes, forfeitures and of and from all other titles, troubles, charges and incumbrances whatsoever had, made, Committed, done or Suffered to bee done by then: the S'd Joshua Hews and Hannah his wife, or either of them, their or either of their heires or assignes, at any time or times before ye Ensealeing hereof and farther that ye Said Joshua Hews and Hannah his wife, their heires and assignes Shall and will from time to time and att all times for ever, hereafter, warrant and Defend the above granted Primisses wth their Appurtainances unto ye Said John fones, his heires and assignes, against all and every P'son or P'sons whatsoever any waies Lawfully claimeing or demanding the Same or any

(79) Part thereof, and lastly the S'd Joshua Hews and Hannah his wife, doe by these Pres'ts make and Constitute the S'd Richard Smith, of Narragansett, afores'd Gent, to bee their Lawfull Attorney in their names and Stead, to Enter Upon ye before granted Land or P'cell of Land or any part thereof, & take possession of ye Same, and after possession had and taken full and Peaceable possession, and Seizin of the Same premisses or any part thereof in ye name of ye whole in their names & Stead, to give and Delliver unto ye Said Jno. fones, his heires and assignes accordinge to ye tenno'r and true meaneing of these presents, and doe hereby covenant to Rattifie and allow whatsoever their S'd Attorney Shall lawfully doe or cause to bee done in and aboute ye Primisses by vertue of these presents; In Wittness whereof ye S'd Joshuah Hews and Hannah his wife, have hereunto Sett their hands and Seales the Eleventh Daye of Novemb'r, Anno Domi One thousand Six hundred Eighty & In the two and thirtieth yeare of ye reigne of our Soveraigne Lord King Charles, the Second over England &c.

Hannah Hews & a Seale.

Joshure Hews & a seale. her X marke.

Signed, Sealed and dellivered
In the presence of us,
Thomas Prentice,
Jireth Bull,
John Howard, Sen'r,
Eliesar Moody.

Josuah Hews and Hannah his wife, personally Appeareing, acknowledged this Instruem't to bee their act and deed before
J. Dudley, Assist.
Dated No'r 12th, 1680.

Know all men by these presents, that I, Alice Hews, Relict, widow of Joshua Hews, late of Boston in New England deceased, for and in Consideration of ye Sum of five pounds of Lawfull money of New England, to mee in hand paid by Capt. John fones, of James Towne in the Collony of Rhoad Island and Providence plantations, have remised, released and quitt Claime, and by these presents doe for mee, heires, Execut'rs, Administrat'rs and assignes, Remise, Release and for ever quitt Claime unto ye Said Jno. Fones, into his quiett and peaceable possession, and Seizen all my Estate, right, title, interest, Dow'r, claime, propertie and Demand, and in & to ye within mentioned tract or P'cell of Land, To have and to hold all my Estate, right, title, Dow'r, Claime, Propertie and Demand whatsoever unto him ye S'd John Fones, his heires and assignes for ever, as wittness my hand and Seale the twelveth day of Novem'r, Anno Dom One thousand Six hundred and Eighty.

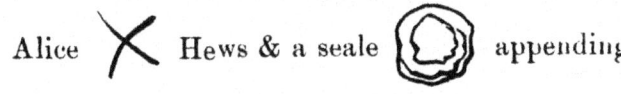

her marke
Alice ╳ Hews & a seale appending

Wittness: John Howard, Sen'r.
Eliesar Moody, Sen'r.

The above written Instruem't was acknowledged by the above named Alice Hews as her act and Deed 12th No'r, 1680. Before mee Tho. Savage, Assist.
Entered upon Record Octo'r 26th, 1686.
P. Jno. Fones, Record'r.

(**80**) Bee it Knowne unto all men by these presents that I, Capt. George Denison, of Stonington in the pequid Country neere New London, and Anne my wife, for and in Consideration of ninetey pounds Sterling money to us in hand by Simon Lynde, of Boston, merchant, well and truely paid, ye receipt whereof wee doe hereby Acknowledge, and thereof, and of every part & parcell thereof, doe hereby fully acquitt and discharge ye Said Simon Lynde, his heires, *Geo. Dennison to Lynde* Execut'rs and Administrat'rs, by these presents have given, granted, bargained, Sold, Enfeaffed and confirmed, and doe hereby give, grant, bargaine, sell, enfeaffe and Confirme unto ye Said Simon Lynde, his heires, Execut'rs, Administrat'rs & assignes for ever, all yt our Necke of lande containeing three hundred acres of lands and meadows, bee it more or less, comonly called Wequapaug Necke or Musquatek, Lyeing in the Pequod countrey, bounded towards the west with a Pond and land granted to the College, haveinge a white oake marked on fower Sides Standing upon a Little hill neare a Small Swamp with a round Rocke very neare itt, betweene the S'd Lands & the College Land & Runing from ye Said tree to ye head of ye Pond Southerly, and bounded towards ye East wth a Brooke caled Weequapaug Brooke, and on the South wth ye Sea, and on ye North wth ye Wilderness as P. the Records of ye Generall Court of ye Massachusetts Collony, and grant wth ye Retturne and Approbation thereof maye appeare, As alsoe all yt our full & whole proportion, Share, Interest, Right, title and claime, In and unto ye Narragansett Countrey, Neantecott and Cowesett Country, made Over to mee the S'd George Denison, and Sundry persons more by Suckquansh, Nenegratt, Scuttuop and Wequakannuitt, alies

Gidion, chiefe Sachems of ye Narragansetts in the behalfe of themselves and ye rest of their Associates as P. ye deede thereof maye more particularly appeare, to have and to hold ye afore bargained Necke of Lande containeing aboute Three hundred Acres as afore said, as alsoe our full and whole Shares, Rights, claimes and Interests In and unto ye Narragansett Countrey, Neantecott and Cowesett Countreys as afore said with all and Singular ye Lands, Meadows, trees, Ponds, Rivers, Brookes, Privilidges, Benefitts, Comonages and appurtainances thereunto bellonging or in any manner or kind from theme to bee had, made, or Received unto him the Said Simon Lynde, his heires, Execut'rs, Administrat'rs and Assignes, to his and their Sole, and onley use, benefitt and behoofe for ever, and I the Said George Denison and Anne my wife, doe for us, our heires, Execut'rs and Administrat'rs, Covenant, Promise and grant to and wth ye Said Simon Lynde his heires, Execut'rs, Administrat'rs and assignes that I ye Said George Denison and Anne my Wife are before ye Ensealeing and Dillevery hereof, the true and Lawfull Owners of The afore bargained Premisses, and have in our Selves full Right and Lawfull Authority to Sell and Dispose ye Same as afore said, and that ye Same and every part and P'cell thereof are free and Cleare from all other or former bargaines, Sales, gifts, grants, titles, Dowers, Claimes or Incumbrances whatsoever, and Shall & will warrant and Defend ye Same, and every part and parcell thereof against all P'son or P'sons whatsoever any waies Claimeing or Demanding ye Same or any part thereof from, by or under us or any of ours and Shall bee ready and willing to doe and passe any further Act or Acts for the further Confirmation of the Premisses unto him ye Said Simon Lynde, his heires, Execut'rs, Administrat'rs and Assignes, as in Law or Equity maye bee desired; In Wittness whereof I the Said George Denison and Anne my wife, have hereunto putt our hands and Seales this two and twentieth day of Octo'r, Anno Domini One thousand Six hundred Seventy and two in ye foure and twentieth yeare of the Raigne of our Soverigne Lord King Charles ye Second.

George Denison & a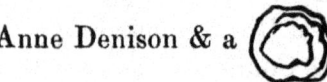

Anne Denison & a

(81) Memorandum the words (hundred) in Reference to ye above said Necke of Land Called Wequapauge necke, containeing aboute three hundred acres and the words (benefitts) were interlined and putt in before the Ensealeing and Dellivery hereof, and afterwards Read over, Signed, Sealed and Dellivered In the presence of us, John Wilson,
Nicho. Page.

Capt. George Denison and Mrs. Anne Denison, acknowledged this writeing to bee their acte and Deed, and ye Said Mrs. Anne Denison, did freely Surrender her Interest of Dowry in the Lands hereby Conveyed, before mee ye 23th of Octob'r, 1672. Daniel Denison.

N'o B Sp 9–10, Entered and Recorded word for word Octob'r 24th, 1672, As Attest.
Isaac Addington, Record'r.

Capt. George Denison and Mrs. Anne Denison, Acknowledged this deede to bee their Acte and deed of Sale this 23 of octob'r, 1672, before mee.
John Winthrop.

This deed on the other Side was Recorded in the publick Records of the Collony of Connecticutt, in the first courte Booke folo 74, this first of Maye, 1673.
P. mee John Allyn, Secret'y.

Entered upon Recorde, Decemb'r 2d, 1686.
P. Jno. Fones Record'r.

Bee it Knowne unto all men by these presents, that I Daniel Gookin of Cambridge in New [England,] Gentlemen, and Mary my wife, for and in Consideration of two hundred and Six pounds of Sterling to us in hand by Symon Lynde, <small>Gookin to Lynde.</small> of Boston, Merchant, well and truely pay'd the receipt whereof wee doe hereby Acknowledge and thereof, and of Every part and parcell thereof doe freely acquitte and discharge ye Said Symon Lynde, his heires, Executo'rs and administrato'rs by these presents being fully Sattisfied and well contented, have and by these Presents doe bargaine and Sell, give, grant, Alien, assigne, Enfeaffe & Confirme unto ye Said Symon Lynde, his heires, Execut'rs, Administrat'rs & assignes for Ever, All yt our farme and houseing thereon being a Necke of Land Sittuate Lyeing and beinge in the Pequod Countrey On Pawcatuck River Neare unto Mr. Thomas Stantons, containeinge aboute five hundred Acres of Land and Meadows, bee it more or Lesse, bounded with ye Said Pawcatuck River westerly, and with the Sound Southerly, with Capt. Thomas Prentice Easterly, and wth ye Wilderness Northerly, as P. ye grant and Records wth ye acts of the generall Courte, held at Boston ye 19th of maye, 1658, to have and to hold ye above granted & bargained Premisses wth all and every the timber, trees, fenceing, privilidges, proffittts, Accommodations, comonagdes and Appurtainces in what Kinde or Nature Soever there unto bellonging or in any manner or wise from them to bee, had, made or Raised unto him ye S'd Symon Lynde, his heires, Execut'rs, Administrat'rs and assignes, and to his and their onley proper use, benefitt and behoofe for ever, and I the said Daniel Gookin and Mary my wife doe for us, our heires, Execut'rs & administrat'rs, Covenant, promise & grante to and with ye Said Symon Lynde, his heires, Executo'rs, Administrato'rs & assignes for Ever, All yt our farme and houseing thereon, being a Necke of Lande Sittuated, Lyeinge and beinge in the Pequod Countrey, on Pawcatuck River Neare unto Mr. Thomas Stantons, containeinge aboute five hundred Acres of Land and Meadows, bee it more or Lesse, bounded with ye Said Pawcatuck River westerly, and with the Sound Southerly, with Capt. Thomas Prentice Easterly, and wth ye Wilderness Northerly, as P. ye graunt and Records wth ye acts of the generall Courte held at Boston ye 19th of maye, 1658, to have and to hold ye above granted & bargained Premisses wth all and every the timber, trees, fenceings, privilidges, proffitts, Accommodations, comonagdes and Appurtainances in what Kinde or Nature Soever, there unto bellonging or in any maneer or wise from them to bee, had, made or Raised unto him ye S'd Symon Lynde, his heires, Executo'rs, Administrato'rs and assignes, and to his and their onley proper use, benefitt and behoofe for ever, and I the Said Daniel Gookin and Mary my wife, doe for us, our heires, Executo'rs & administrato'rs, Covenant, promise & graunte to and with ye Said Symon Lynde, his heires, Executo'rs, administrato'rs

(82) and assignes, that I the Said Daniel Gookin and Mary my wife, are before the Ensealeing and dellivery hereof, ye true and Lawfull owners of the afore bargained premisses and have in our Selves full Right & Lawfull Authority to Sell and Dispose ye Same as afore Said, and yt the Same & every part and parcell thereof are free and Cleere from all other or former Bargaines, Sales, gifts, graunts, Dowries titles, claimes or Incumbrances Whatsoever, and Shall and will Warrant and defend the Same and Every part and parcell thereof against all P'son or P'sons whatsoever any waies Claimeing or demanding ye Same or any part thereof by, from or under mee the Said Daniel or Mary my wife, and Shall bee ready & willing to doe any further acte or actes for ye further and Legall Confirmation of the premisses unto him ye Said Symon Lynde, his heires, Executo'rs, Administrato'rs and assignes, as in Law or Equity might bee desired; In Wittness whereof I the Said Daniel Gookin and Mary my wife, have hereunto putt o'r hands and Seales this Sixth day of february Anno Domi 1671, In ye fower and twentieth

yeare of ye Reigne of o'r Soveraigne Lord King Charles the Second.

Daniel Gookin & a

Mary Gookin & a

Sealed and Dellivered In presence of
Edward Michellson,
Samuel Green.

Acknowledged by the Worr's, Daniel Gookin, Esq'r and Mrs Mary Gookin his wife, to bee their Joint Acte and Deed and by them Signed and Sealed this 6th of february, 1671, before
Thomas Danforth, Assist.

Booke 7th p 316-17. Entered and Recorded word for word and Compared therewith this 6th of 1st m'o, 1671-72, as attest.

ffree Grace Bendall, Cler.

This Deed May 1st, 1673, was Entered in the publicke Records of the Colloney of Conecticott, in the first Courte booke fo. 74.

P. mee John Allyn, Sect'ry.

Acknowledged by mr. Daniel Gookin, to bee his Act and deed Octo'r 24th, 1672, before mee.

John Winthrop.

Entered upon Record, Decemb'r 2d, 1686.

P. Jno. Fones, Record'r.

Know all men by these presents, that I, Amos Richardson of Boston and my wife, for and in Consideration of tenn pounds of Lawfull money of New England to us in hand by Symon Lynde of Boston, Merchant, well and truely paid, the receipt whereof wee doe hereby acknowledge, and thereof and of every part and parcell thereof doe fully

Amos Richardson to Lynde.

acquitt and Discharge the Said Symon Lynde, and his by
these presents have and hereby doe fully thereby & absolutely
Bargaine, Sell, give, graunt, assigne, Enfeaffe and Confirme
unto the Said Symon Lynde, his heires, Executo'rs, Administrato'rs and assignes for ever, all that our one hundred acres
of Land Sittuate and being on Squamococke or Pawcatuck
Necke, on the East Side of the Southerly End thereof fifty
acres of which was by a graunt to

(83) us from
the towne of Stoningtone, and fifty acres which was graunted
unto John fitch, the Said one hundred Acres being layd out
and Surveyed with a greater Parcell by Epraham Minor and
John Frink, being bounded as ye Returne of the Said Sur-
veryo'rs, and Recorded in ye Records of Stonington, doe
make appeare, To have and to hold ye aforesaid One hundred Acres of Lande with all Singular ye Meadows, timber
woods, prividges and Appurtainances with, bellonging or
in any wise appurtaining or of Benefitts or prcffith
from theme to bee had, made or Raised unto him ye Said
Symon Lynde, his heires, Executo'rs, Administrato'rs and assignes, and to his and their Sole use, benefitt and Behoofe for
Ever, and I, the Said Amos Richardson, and Mary, my wife,
doe for our heires, Executo'rs & administrato'rs covenant,
promise and graunt to and with ye Said Symon Lynde and
his by these presents that I, the Said Amos Richardson and
Mary, my wife, are before the Ensealeing and dellivery hereof the true and Sole owners of the afore Bargained premisses, and have in o'r Selves full power and Right to Sell
and Dispose ye Same as afore Said, and yt the Same and
every part and parcell thereof are free and Cleere from all
former or other Bargaines, gifts, graunts, Titles, charges or
Incumbrances whatsoever, and Shall and will warrant and
defend the Same and Every part thereof against all P'son or
P'sons Lawfully Claimeing or demanding the Same, hereby
giveing and dellivering Possession, Livery and Seizen thereof

unto the Said Symon Lynde; In Wittness Whereof wee have here unto putt our hands and Seales this thirteenth day of Aug'st, Anno 1677, in the 29th yeare of the Reigne of o'r Soveraigne Lord, King Charles the Second.

Amos Richardson &

Mary Richardson & a

Signed, Sealed and Dellivered in the Presence of us,

Stephen Richardson,
Lydia Richardson.

This deed above written was owned to bee their owne proper acte and deed, by the Subscribers this 13th day of Aug'st, 1677, before mee,

Thomas Minor, Comis'r.

This Deed of Sale on the other Side, this was Entered in Stonington booke of Records, in page ye 83d, this 13th day of Aug'st, 1677.

P. mee John Stanton, Record'r.

Entered upon Record this 2d Decemb'r, 1686.

P. Jno. Fones, Record'r.

Know all men by these Presents that I, Stephen Richardson of Stonington, In New England, yeoman, for and in Consideration of three pounds value in money to mee and *Stephen Richard-* my wife, Lydia Richardson, in hand, well and *son to Lynde.* truly paid by Symon Lynde of Boston, in New England, merchant, the Receipt whereof wee doe hereby acknowledge, and thereof doe fully acquitt the Said Lynde and his by these presents have and hereby doe give, graunt, Bargaine, Sell, assigne, Enfeaffe and confirme unto ye Said Symon Lynde, his heires, Executo'rs, administrato'rs and Assignes by these presents, Thirty Acres of Land Sittuate and being on Squamococke or Pawcatuck Necke on the East Side of the

Southerly End thereof graunted by ye towne of Stonington, and layd out & Surveyed (with a greater parcell) by Ephraim Minor and John Frink, Bounded as by the Returnes of the Said Survaiyo'rs and Records.

(84) In the towne of Stonington doe make appeare to have and to hold the aforesaid thirty Acres of Land with all and Singular, ye Meadows, Timber, Woods, Comonages, benefitts, Privilidges and Appurtainances thereunto Bellonging or in any wise appurtaineing unto him ye Said Symon Lynde, his heires, Executo'rs, Administrato'rs and assignes, and to his & their Sole and onley use, benefitt and behoofe for ever, and I the S'd Stephen Richardson and Lydia Richardson my wife, doe hereby for us, our heires. Executo'rs and Administrato'rs covenant, promise and graunt to and with ye Said Symon Lynde and his, vt I the Said Stephen Richardson & Lydia my wife, are ye true and proper Owners of the aforeS'd Land at and before the Ensealeing and dellivery hereof, and have in o'r Selves full pow'r, Right and Lawfull Authoritie to Sell and Conveaye the same as afore Said, and yt ye Same is free from all former or other Bargaines, gifts, grants Titles, charges and Incumbrances whatsoever, and Shall & will Warrant and Defend ye Same against all P'son or P'sons Lawfully claimeing Or demanding ye Same or any part or parcell thereof, hereby giveing & dellivering possession, Seizen and hereby thereof unto ye S'd Symon Lynde; In Wittness whereof wee have hereunto putt o'r hands and Seales this thirteenth day of August, Anno 1677 in the 29th yeare of ye Raigne of o'r Soveraigne Lord King Charles the Second.

Stephen Richardson & a

Lydia Richardson & a

Signed, Sealed and Dellivered
In the Presence of us,
Amos Richardson,
Tho. Minor.

This deed above written was owned by the Subscrib'r to bee their owne proper Acte and Deed the 13th of Aug'st, 1677 before mee.

Tho. Minor, Comis'r.

This above written deed was Entered in Stonington booke of Records, In page ye 81, this thirteenth of Aug'st 1677.
P. mee. John Stanton, Record'r.

Entered upon Record, decemb'r 2d, 1686.
P. Jno Fones, Record'r,

Thomas Bell of Stonington, taylor, in Consideration of twelve pounds, fifteen Shillings, money in hand paid him by Symon Lynde of Boston, merchant, hath given, graunted, Sold and confirmed unto ye Said Symon Lynde and his for *Thom. Bell to Lynde.* ever One hundred and twenty Acres of [sic] Land lyeing In and upon Squamacocke or Pawcatuck necke, viz., Ninety acres thereof Layd out upon ye Said Necke by Epraham Minor and John Frinke, Survaiyo'rs of Stonington, and butted and bounded as by their Returne Recorded in ye towne booke of Records the 15th of June, 1675, may appeare, and thirty acres of Land more Lyeing at the Northerly End of the Said necke Layd out unto Robert Stanton, Butted and bounded as By the Returnes of the Survaiyo'rs, Recorded in the afore said Towne booke of Records at Stonington maye appeare, To have and to hold ye aforesaid

(**85**) One hundred and twenty acres of Land as above mentioned, together with all and Singular, the privilidges, members rights, Comonages, benefitts and Appurtainances in any Kinde or maner whatsoever, which doe or maye belonge unto ye Same, unto ye

Said Symon Lynde, his heires, Executo'rs, administrat'rs and assignes for ever to his the Said Lynde and his heires, & benefitt and behoofe, and hee the Said Thomas Bell for him and his, doth hereby Covenant and promise, & graunt to & wth the S'd Lynde, and his, yt hee the Said Bell is before ye Ensealeing and dellivery hereof, the true owner of the aforesaid Lands and hath in himselfe full power and right to Alienate and sell yt Same as aforesaid, and that ye Same is free and cleare from all other bargains, Sales, gifts, grauntes, dowers Incumbrances whatsoever, and yt hee, ye Said Thomas Bell Shall and will warrant, and defend ye Same and Every part thereof unto ye Said Lynde, and his, against all P'son or P'sons whatsoever, and further yt that hee, the Said Thomas Bell, Shall and will at all tyme or tymes, give unto the Said Lynde or his, more full and ample assurance and confirmation of the afore bargained premises, as in Law or Equity can be desired or Required. In Witness whereof hee, the Said thomas Bell, hath hereunto putt his hand and Seale this 14th day or Octob'r, Anno 1675,

Thomas Bell & a

Signed, Sealed and Delivered
 by the Said Thomas Bell in
  the presence of us,
  John Marsh,
   her mark

  Mary Marsh,
   her mark.

  Hannah H I Johnson.

This deed above written was owned by Thomas Bell to bee his owne proper Deed and act, this 6th of Novem'br 1676.
  before mee   Thomas Minor, Bomis'r.
 This deed of Tho. Bell to mr. Symon Lynde is Entered in Stonington booke of Records, page 82, this 13th Aug's 1677.   P. mee, John Stanton, Record'r.
 John Marsh, aged aboute 28 years, and mary Marsh, aged about 28 years deposed yt they saw Thomas Bell Signe, Seale as his Acte and deed, delivered ye above written deed Taken upon Oath, the 4th of 3d mo. before mee
         Thomas Clarke, Comis'r.
Entered upon Record Decemb'r 2d, 1686.
        P. Jno. Fones, Record'r.

Mr. Lyndes;
 Kind S'r, after respects presented, you maye bee pleased to take Notice that I have done my uttmost of my Indeav'ors for ye well Settlem'ts of yo'r Affaires, and by the Industrey of ye Scrivenay'rs and willingness in all Respects to Contrive for your best Advantage. Jno. Gallop refused to show them ye fifty acres you bought, Which putt us to a nonplus, hee telling us the night before that hee would doe Itt and went wth us the next morning upon the Necke, but no Sooner there but his mind changed Soe yt wee could not goe Soe high as wee Intended, however Run ye line to yt mark Sett above ye house, and Stated whilst you were there, and Soe upon a Straite Line to Mr. Hayehews as was intended, but there fell to bee 24 acres more than wee had purchased, the Surveyo'rs was forced to Laye out part of the Beach for Land, Thomas Bell Sayiug he would

(86) Else have it layd out for a Lott which Occasioned the thing to bee done for his prevention, Whereupon the Survayo'rs thought fitt to waite to ye Court Supposeing they would have allowed yt 24 acres in Consideration of the Beach,

but Jno. Gallop, Senio'r, being at ye Court pleaded yt 2 hummucks and beach and some other addition might bee Reserved for a fishing trade, the Court willing to harken did Say you Should have Land without your Line or above it alowed for it which I ordered could not bee being already taken up, suppose Deacon Park's did dilliver you said Message, the Courte Seemed to owne noe thinge could bee done without yo'r Consent y'r you maye bee assured ye Survayo'rs and my Selfe have Acted to the uttmost of o'r Skill not Else but yt I rest yo'rs to Serve.

Amos Richardson.

Att Mr. Smith's, June ye 18th, 75, Wickford.

Know all men by these presents, that I Richard Smith, of Narragansett in the Kings Province, doe by these Presents *Richard Smith to John Briggs,* for and in Consideration of Twenty fife pounds in hand received from John Briggs, of Narragansett afore S'd, have granted, bargained and sould, Alienated & conveyed unto ye S'd John Briggs, his heires, Executo'rs, Administrato'rs & Assignes all & singular, the land formerly belonging to Ruben Willis, which I bought in England from his father & Mother, William and Susana Hixe they haveing order from Ruben Willis to make Sale of the Same, it lyeing & being scituated in Narragansett countrey, Containing by Estimation fiffty seven Acres more or less, Bounded on ye East by fife hundred Acres of land not laid out as it in ye Northward purchase, on ye west bounded by ye common, on ye North with ye high way, on ye south by ye land of Samuel Waight, all which the rights & privilidges thereunto belonging or in any wise apertaining, I doe bargaine and Sell unto ye S'd John Briggs, his heires, Executo'rs, Administrat'rs and assignes from me, my heires, Executo'rs, Administrato'rs & Assignes to have & to hould, possess and Injoy for Ever without any manner of Chalenge, Let or claime from or by or under mee, or by my cause or meanes whatsoever; in Wittness of ye Promise above written, the above s'd Richard Smith hath hereunto sett his hand & affixed his seale this Eleaventh day of January, Ano Do 1672.

Rich'd Smith & a seale.

Signed, Sealed and dellivered
   in ye Presents of
    Henry Teeppitts,
    his *H* marke
    John Greene.

This above written deed was Entred and Recorded in ye Publick Records of his majes'ts Colony of Rhode Island and Providence plantations, in ye 163 page of ye Booke of Land Evidences, ye 8th of August, 1674 as Attests.

John Sanford, Record'r.

Rochester, June 28, 1686.

The above written Deed was acknowledged by Majo'r Richard Smith, before me ye Subscriber being one of his Majes'tis Councill for his Territory & Dominion in New England. R'd Wharton.

Entered upon Record, february 11th, 1686-7.

P. Jno. Fones, Record'r.

(87) To all CHRISTIAN PEOPLE to whom this present deed of Sale shall come, Richard Smith, of Rochester in ye ings Province in New England, Esq'r and Ester his wife send

Richard Smith to Wm. Palmer. Greeting; Know yee that ye said Richard Smith and Ester his wife, for and in Consideration of ye Sume of thirty pounds of lawfull money of New England, to them in hand paid at and before ye Ensealeing & delivery of these presents by William Palmer, late of ye Island of Barbados, (gunsmith) well & truely paid, The receipt thereof they doe hereby acknowledge, and themselves therewith satisfied, contented and paid, Have given, granted, bargained, sold, Enfeaffed and confirmed, And by these presents doe fully & absolutely give, grant, bargaine, Sell Enfeaffe & confirme unto ye S'd William Palmer, his heires, Execut'rs & Administrat'rs & assignes, all their right, Title and Interest in and unto a certaine tract or parcell of land situate, lyeing & being in ye Township of Rochester afore S'd, containing forty Acres, Bounded on ye South or Southerly by Anoquatuckett river (so called,) and Westerly, Northerly & Easterly upon ye land of ye afore S'd Richard Smith. The length of S'd land to be one hundred and Sixty rod upon ye S'd river, and forty rods in Breadth with all rights, privilidges and appurtainances to ye same belonging, To have and to hold ye afore bargained Premisses and all & Every Part thereof, Together wth all ye rights, privilidges & appurtenances to ye same belonging or in any wise Apurtaining unto ye S'd William Palmer, his heires & assignes, and To ye only proper use, Benefit & behoofe of him, ye S'd William Palmer, his heires, Executo'rs, Administrator's & assignes for Ever, In such large and and ample sort, manner & forme as they ye S'd Richard & Ester may grant, convey & assure ye same, And ye S'd Richard Smith & Ester his wife, doth hereby covenant, promise & grant to & wth ye S'd William Palmer, his heires & assignes, That ye afore bargained Premisses, wth all ye rights & privilidges and appurtenances thereof as afore S'd against them, ye S'd Richard & Ester, his wife, their heires, Executo'rs & Administrato'rs, or any for, by or under them, or any of them shall & will warrant & for Ever defend by these Presents, And doe oblidge themselves to deliver full possession and Seizen of ye within bargained Premises unto ye S'd William Palmer, his heires or Assignes; In Witness whereof the s'd Richard Smith and Ester Smith, his wife, have hereunto set their hands & seales The third of may Anoy'e Domy'e one thousand six hundred Eighty & seaven, And in ye third yeare of ye reigne of o'r Soveraign Lord, James ye Second, King of England, Scotland, ffrance & Ireland, Defender of ye faith, &c.

Rich'd Smith &  a seale.

Ester Smith & a seale.

Signed, Sealed & Delivered
in ye presents of us
    Lodowick Updick,
        Abigall A Π Newton,
            her marke

Richard Smith Esq'r and Ester Smith, his wife, ye Persons above mentioned, did declare the above written Instruement to be their Reall act & deed before

        Jno. Fones, Justicia Pacis.
Entered upon Record, May ye 12th, 1687.
        P. Jno. Fones, Record'r.

To all Christian People wherever these presents shall come, Samuell Wilson of ye Towne of Rochester in ye Kings Province in New England, Send Greeting; Know yee that I ye said Samuell Wilson, for and in Consideration of ye sume of thirty pounds, currant money of New England, to mee in hand before the Edsealeing & delivery of these presents, well & truely paid by Henry Bull of Rochester afore Sd, The receipt whereof to full content & satisfaction I doe hereby acknowledge, Have given, granted, Bargained, Sould, Enfeaffed & confirmed, and by these presents doe ffully and absolutely give, grant, Bargaine, sell, enfeaffe and confirme unto ye S'd Henry Bull, his heires, Executo'rs Administrato'rs & Assignes, all my right, title & Interest in all that parcell of land scituate, lyeing & being in ye Township of Rochester afore S'd, Containing one hundred Acres, the Breadth of S'd Tract to Containe one hundred & tenn Rod and ye length thereof to make and compleat ye S'd Sume of one hundred Acres, Bounded Northerly & westerly upon ye land

(88) land of Samuell Wilson afore mentioned, Southerly upon ye land of Capt. Samuell Seawell, and Easterly upon a highway, with all rights, privilidges & appurtainances to ye same belonging or in any wise appertaining. To have & to

hold the afore bargained Premisses and all & Every Part & Parcell thereof wth all ye rights, privilidges and appurtainances thereunto belonging unto him ye S'd Henry Bull, his heires, Executo'rs, Administrato'rs and assigness for Ever, And to his [and] their only proper use and behoofe in Such large & ample sort, manner & forme, as I ye S'd Samuel Wilson, may grant, convey and assure ye same, And that I doe hereby covenant, for me & my heires, Executo'rs & Administrato'rs, That ye afore granted Premisses with all ye right, privilidges & appurtainances thereof, as afore S'd unto him ye S'd Henry Bull, his heires, & assignes against me, my heires, Executo'rs & Administrato'rs, or any claimeing by, for or under mee, I shall & will warrant and for Ever defend by these Presents, And doe oblige my selfe, my heires, Executors & Administrato'rs to give delivery & seizing of ye S'd Tract of land before by these presents granted unto the S'd Henry Bull, his heires, Executo'rs, Admininistrato'rs or assignes; In Wittness whereof I ye S'd Samuell Wilson have hereunto sett my hand and seale the 29th day of Aprill, An'o Dom'e one thousand six hundred Eighty & Seaven, And in the third yeare of ye Raigne of o'r Soveraigne Lord James ye second by the grace of God, King of great Britaine ffrance & Ireland, Defender of ye faith &c.

        Samuell Willson &  a seale.

Signed, Sealed & Delivered
 in ye presents of us,
  James Coggeshall,
  Nathonall Osband,
 The *Im* marke of
  Thomas Marshall.

Samuell Wilson ye above named disposer & seller of ye tract of land above mentioned, did apeare & declare ye above written Instruem't to be his Reall act & Deed the 16th day of May, 1687, before us,

Rich'd Smith,
Jno. Fones, } Justices of ye Peace.

Entered upon Record, May ye 25th, 1687.

P. Jno. Fones, Record'r.

Articles of Agreement had made and Concluded on the last day of Novemb'r in the Second yeare of the Reigne of o'r Sovereigne Lord James the Second over England &c. Any'e Domy't 1686, Betweene Thomas Mumford, Peleg Mumford and John Shelden, all of the Towne of Rochester in ye Kings Province or Narragansett Countrey in New England, And Samuell Mead of the Towne of Warwick in the Colony of Rhode Island and Providence Plantations in New England afore Said, Witnesseth that whereas the S'd Persons above Named haveing Joyned themselves mutually in Partership to Erect, build and and sett up a grist mill in ye Township of Rochester afore S'd upon a river called and Knowne by ye Name of Mattatuxett, upon ye land now in Possession of Bethia Palmer, Widow and Relict of George Palmer, late Deceased, The which S'd Mill being by them erected, built and Sett up as afore S'd at ye proper costs and Charge of ye S'd Thomas Mumford, Peleg Mumford, John Sheldon and Samuel Mead, afore S'd Each of them Beareing an Equall part and proportion thereof, doe agree that ye S'd Mill Shall be well finished and a fulling Mill anexed and Joyned to ye S'd Grist Mill at their proper costs and Charge, Each one Beareing his part and proportion which being done, performed and finished, The S'd Mills to Belong unto the S'd Thomas Mumford, Peleg Mumford, John Sheldon and Samuel Mead, their and Every of their heires and Assignes on Equall part (that is to say) a fourth part to Each Partner, to be and Remaine to Each and Every of them so long as ye S'd Mills shall Endure. In Witness whereof the parties above Named have wth free and Joynt Consent, Sett to their hand & Seales the day and yeare first above written,

Thomas Mumford & a Seale,

Peleg Mumford & a seale,

John Shelden & a seale,

Samuell Mead & a seale.

Signed, Sealed and declared to be the reall act and agreem't of ye Subscribers in Presence of us,
    Ephram More,
    John Fones.

Entered upon Record Sept'r 17th, 1688.
                P. Jno. Fones, Record'r.

(89) To all People to whom these presents shall come; Know yee, that I James Updike of Boston, Shipwright, for and in Consideration of ye sume of Eleven pounds New England money, to me in hand paid before the Ensealing and Delivery of these presents By ffrancis Brinley of Newport in Rhode Island, The Receipt whereof I doe hereby acknowledge And off the same, and of every part thereof doe hereby fully acquitt, Release and discharge the said ffrancis Brinley, his heires and Assignes Have granted, Bargained, aliened, Sold, Enfeaffed and Confirmed, And by these Presents doe fully freely and Absolutely grant, Bargain, Sell, Enfeaffe and confirme unto ye s'd ffrancis Brinley, his heires and assignes for Ever, all my Right, Title and Interest in and unto certaine lands in ye Narragansett Countrey (Lying to ye southward of my unkle, mr. Richard Smiths dwelling house formerly called ye Trading house wch was left as a

Legasy in ye Last will and Testament of my Grand father, mr. Richard Smith, Deceased) as Relation being had to ye S'd will may more Amply appeare, And also all and Singular, the Rights, privilidges and Appurtenances to ye Same Belonging or in any wise Appurtaineing To Have and to hold the S'd lands and Premisses so Bequeathed unto me as afore s'd, Together with all and Singular ye rights, Privilidges and Appurtenances afore Recited unto him the s'd ffrancis Brinley, his heires and Assignes To ye onley Proper use and behoofe of him the said ffrancis Brinley, his heires and Assignes for Ever, And I the said James Updike for me, my heires, Executo'rs & Administrato'rs doe hereby covenant and Promise to and with ye S'd ffrancis Brinley, his heires, Executo'rs, Administrato'rs and Assignes, That at ye time of the Ensealeing and delivery of these presents, I am Seized of ye S'd lands and Premisses herein above Granted & Sold in a good and Indefeaseable Estate in ffee Simple, and have full power and lawfull authority to Bargaine and Sell ye Same in manner and forme as is in these Presents above Expressed, And I ye S'd James Updike, the S'd lands and premisses wth all and Singular, ye appurtenances above Expressed to be hereby Granted and Sold unto him ye S'd ffrancis Brinley, his heires and Assignes against me, my heires and Assignes or any Person or Persons claimeing by, from or under mee will warrant and for ever defend by these presents; In Witness whereof I have hereunto Set my hand [and] Seale the twentieth day of March, in ye Six and thirtieth yeare of the Reigne of o'r Soveraign Lord Charles ye Second, by ye Grace of God, of England, Scotland, ffrance & Ireland King, Defender of ye faith &c. Annq'e Domq'e 1684.

James Updike & seale

Sealed and Delivered
  in ye Presents of
    John Prentis,
    Wm. Brenley.
  Mr. William Brinley appeared before me this 23th day of octob'r, 1686, in South hold and made oath that he saw James Updike Signe, Seale and deliver this as his act and deed to wch he was a wittness and subscribed.
                                Teste Asa Arnold.
  decemb'r 14th, 1686.
  Entered and Recorded in ye first booke of Records for Kings Province N. England & in ye 2d and 3'd pages thereof.
                             Ed. Randolph, Register.
  Boston, decemb'r 14th, 1686.
  James Updike above Written, personally appeared before me, one of his Maj'ties Councill in this his Maj'ties Territory and Dominion of New England, and Acknowledged this Instruem't of Conveyance to be his voluntary act and Deed for ye uses therein mentioned.
                      Ed. Randolph, Reg's in Rochester.
  Entered upon Record ye 9th day of August 1692.
                            P. John Fones, Record'r.

Wee whose names are under written doth acknowledge to have received from Richard Wharton, Attourney or Scrivener for Mr. Richard Smith, of Narragansett, forty pounds in money, being what remaines in ye hands of and due from mr. Smith for land Sold ye S'd Smith lying in ye Narragansett countrey By Jonathan Atherton, Administrator to Maj'r Humphrey Atherton, Deceased, and wee doe hereby oblige ourselves, o'r heires, Executo'rs & Administrato'rs That wee will discharge ye Said Smith, any ye Lands so Sold for ye afore said sume, and acquitt our Respective Interest to all and every parcell of afore s'd land, also for ever to Release ye s'd Smith from all Claimes, demands and obligations with

Reference to any or all ye afore s'd Estate, and doe respectively promise and oblige our Selves, heires, Executo'rs & Administrato'rs to repay to any of ye children of S'd Maj'r Atherton to whom ye Same may be due what wee doe receive more than our proper due from ye S'd Smith, Witness our hands and Seales twenty Eight of November, 1676.

    Jonathan Atherton a seale seale.

    obadiah Swift and a seale  seale.

    Thomas Bird and a seale  seale.

    John Clarke and a seale  seale.

Sealed ann Delivered
 in ye presence of
  Wm. Taylor,
  Charles Tidgett.

Boston, Octob'r 18th, 1686, Capt. Charles Tidgett appeared before me ye Subscriber being one of his Maj'ties Councill, for his Territory & Dominion of N. E., and made oath that hee saw mr. Jonathan Atherton, obadiah Swift, Thomas Bird & John Clarke, Signe, Seale ye Instruem't within as their act & deed, and that he witness thereto Subscribed his name, I declare and certify that I have certaine knowledge & rememberance of ye payment of money within mentioned to ye S'd Persons being in my presence, and by my order have Paid Capt. Tidgett, I having order from S'd Smith above mentioned.

            R'd Wharton.

Entered upon Record ye 9th day of August.
         P. J. F. Record'r.

(90) This deed of Sale made ye first day of January, in ye Twenty fourth yeare of ye Reigne of our Sovereigne Lord Charles ye second, King of great Brittaine, ffrance & Ireland, Defender of ye faith &c. Annoq'e Domq'e 1671-72, Wittnesseth That I Anashuecot, chiefe Sachem and heire properly of ye land called quckeset, in ye Colony of Rhode Island and Providence Plantations in ye Kings Province or Narragansett Countrey in New England, Together with ye volentary & free consent of Wampkegge and Ompamiatt my two Brothers, and Seecomp, Tyecuecsha & Nammeash my three sons, for divers good causes & considerations, us hereunto moveing as also for a valueable Sume in hand by us received, have Bargained and Sold, and by these Presents doe for us, our heires, Executo'rs & Administrato'rs, Bargaine, Sell, Assigne, Surrender and make over unto John Greene, Thomas Waterman, John Andrew, Henry Tybits, John Briggs all of Narragansett afore'sd, and John Fones of Quononaqutt in ye Colony of Rhode Island & Providence Plantations, as above S'd, a certaine tract of land lyeing & being in Quahessett or Narragansett countrey afore S'd, being bounded as followeth, on ye East from ye house of John Andrew before nominated Extending along ye Rhode that leadeth towards New london, on ye west Syde thereof so farr as ye Rock by ye house of William Costen the which is called Interpretation ye Devills foot, and from that Rock to Extend on a strait line westward over ye river, ye great river & meadow called Pasutat, thence to a Rock on ye west Syde of that river & meadow, and from ye westermost parte of that Rock on a strait line North to a river, the biggest branch thereof which river runs downe to Maskchechuaug river, and from that Maskchechnaeg river along ye path on a strait line south Eastward to ye river called Potowome river, Butting upon land wch was laid out to John Gould so high in ye river as ye salt water floweth, and from that part to ye river alone ye s'd river as it runeth to John Andrews house afore S'd, The which S'd tract of land with all and Singular, ye privilidges, proprieties & ap-

purtenances therein, thereon or to any part or parcell of it appurtaineing or belonging, I the afore S'd Anashusett together with my two Brothers, Wampkegge & Ompamiatt, and my three sons Seecomp, Tyecuecsha & Nammeash, have sold, Assigned, Surrendered & made over, and lawfull possession thereof given to ye afore S'd John Greene, Thomas Waterman, John Andrew, Henry Tybits, John Briggs & John Fones, for them, their heires, Executo'rs, Administrato'rs & Assignes peaceably to possess & Enjoy for Ever, without any let or Molestation or any laying claime thereto or any part thereof for, by or under any Right or Title of us ye afore s'd Awashueset, Wampkegge, Ompamiatt, Seecomp, Tyecuecsha & Nammeash, our heires. Execut'rs, Administrato'rs or Assignes or any other, and any pretence whatsoever wee being ye Sole heires & proprietors of ye Premisses afore s'd, Giving, granting & confirming ye same To ye afore S'd John Greene, Thomas Waterman, John Andrew, Henry Tybits, John Briggs & John Fones, their heires, Executors, Administrato'rs and Assignes for Ever, to possess & Enjoy as their due Right, propriety & Interest, and for ye rattification & confirmation of this our act and Deed wee have Enanimously with one consent Sett our hands & Seales The day and yeare first above written.

memo'edum before signeing & sealing hereof being mistaken in the name of ye third it was Interlined, Tyecuecsha and also that Namoush being ye Eldest son by misinformation was placed last wch will not be altered.

      Anashuecut ✗ his marke

      Wamphagge   his marke

Absolome Counsellor.

  his ◯ marke

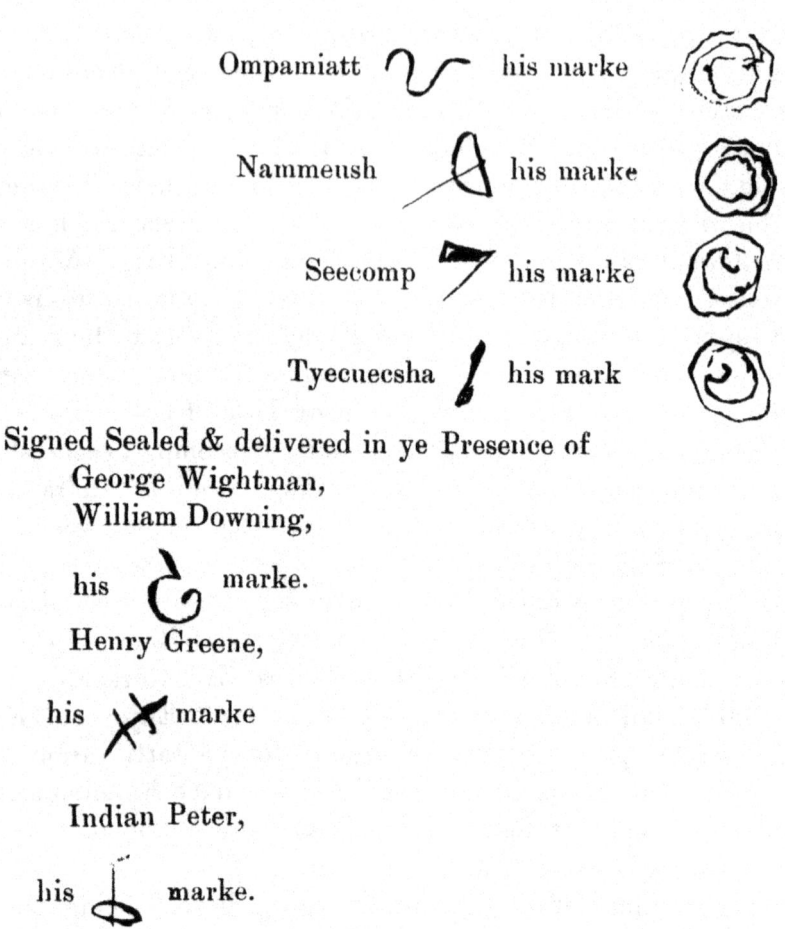

Signed Sealed & delivered in ye Presence of
George Wightman,
William Downing,

his   marke.

Henry Greene,

his   marke

Indian Peter,

his   marke.

Entered upon Record ye 24th day of July, 1703,

Newport on Rhode Island, January 3th, 1677-8, Personally appeared Before me an Indian called Absolom, and declared as followeth, Viz.: that he had been a Counsillor unto ye Indian Sachem Moseupp and that he was knowing unto a Bargaine and Saile of land, that ye Indian sachem called Anashuecutt, made unto John Greene, Henry Tibbetts, John Fones, Thomas Waterman, John Andrew & John Briggs, and was present at ye time of ye Signing & Delivering of ye Deed of Saile for ye Same, and when possession of ye S'd land was delivered, and that ye sevearall bounds & lines of ye S'd land was justly & truely explained unto ye Sachem Anashuecut as it is Expressed in ye Deed of Saile Bearing date first day of Janua'y, 1671, Being now Read & Interpreted unto me, and that ye sevearall lines of ye lands as is in ye S'd Deed of Saile Expressed, was to run Straight only ye line upon Masquechuaug river, and further saith that Anashuecutt, his two Brothers, with his three sons did also Sell ye S'd lands & sett their hands unto ye S'd Deed of Saile unto which I am a witnes, The S'd Absolome further declared that he thanked God he had this opertunity to declare ye truth before Authority [A] nashuecutt, being conveyed out of ye country, Washaucutt his brother nor their sonnes never having sold any part of it before unto any English, Mr. Browne being left as as [sic] a Guardian by his father Tocomminon that ye other Indian sachems should not deprive him of his land.

This above written was Interpreted as ye Indian spake
Before Peleg Sanford, Assist.

Daniel Stanton aged aboute thirty one yeares, upon his Engagement Testifieth that he did truly & Justly Interpret what is above written, that was Spoken by ye Indian Absolom, Taken ye 3th January, 1677-8.
Before Peleg Sanford, Assistant.

Entered upon Record ye 24th day of July, 1703.
P. J. F.

170

Note. the following items are found on the first blank leaves in this book which explaine themselves by the text.

The Compiler.

Acco't of Disburse by Sundry proprieot'rs of ye Mortgage & other Lands at ye Narragansett.

March 9, Then Ordered for defraying mr. Saffins Charges Conecticutt, 10 Shillings each share. p'd Viz.

    Capt. Waite Winthrop,
    Elisha Hutchinson,   0-10-00
    Jno. Williams for mr. Alcocke.

Oct. 5, 1679, Expenses at ye Committys Meeting at Woodcocks.

Capt. Rich Smith,	1-00-00
mr. John Saffin,	1-00-00
Elisha Hutchinson,	1-00-00
mr. Amos Richerson,	
mr. Browne.	

An Acco't of Disbursements by sundry proprietors of Nor'r & South Tracts, Aug. 5, when Ordered & Agreed in paym't for bill Exchange £19-5-8 sent to mr Harris, bought of Elias Parkman for £22-5-3, p'd Viz. by,

Capt. Waite Winthrop,	3-8-6
mr. Rich Wharton,	1-14-3
mr. Will Taylor,	
mr. Rich Smith &	6-17-00
mr. Jno. Viall,	
mr. ffra. Brenley,	3-8-6
mr. Jno. Saffin,	3-8-6
Elisha Hutchinson,	3-8-6
	22-5-3

171

Northern & Southern Tract of Land   Dr.

I finde in a paper this written, Charges upon the southern business to be borne by ye whole Comp'a 8'm Sixty-two.

Major Atherton,	5-00-00
mr. Smith,	10-00-00
Capt. Hudson,	20-00-00
E. Hutchinson,	10-00-00
mr. Rich Smith, Jun'r.	1-10-00
	36-10-00

Mortgage Land is   Dr.

I finde in a paper this Account of Peage yt was paid at first to Gov. Winthrop being 735 fathems by   fathems.

Edward Hutchinson,	74
Capt. Wm. Hudson,	57 3-4
Capt. Denison, mr. Tho. Stanton, (Stoningtown, & his son,)	120
Maj'r Atherton,	42 3-4
mr. Alcock,	40 3-4
Gov'r Winthrop, Capt. Lord, mr. Richeson, } Conecticutt,	120
mr. Smiths.	280
	735

more Edw. Hutchinson paid severall as per his booke besides ye said above £25-19-4.

Note. The following is found in the last 480 leaves of this Proprietors book.   The Compiler.

(1*) At a Comisoners Court, held at Wickford, in Conecticot Collonie.

22 August, 1672.

Present mr. Sam'l Willis, Edward Hutchinson, Capt. Wm. Hudson.

Edward Hutchinson was apointed recorder of ye Court.

The Court being set, John Johnson being called appeared to prosecute according to his bond, ye wife of Edmond Cosons for felloniusly takeing out of his house divers goods & other misdemeanors, ye wife of Edmund Cosons also appeared, but by reason some witnesses in ye caise was not p'sent, ye caise was deferred until next morning and warant sent for ye witnesses then to appeare, presently after this there came a writeing to ye Court sent by one upon ye magestraites of Roade Island, termed ye offercer wch was as followeth, To mr. Samuel Willis, Esq'r, Capt. Edward Hutchinson & Capt. William Hudson and all others whom it may concerne Gent'lm.

We being informed yt yo'r selves by Authority of ye Collony of Conecticot are intended to hould a Court & Exercise Authority wth in ye Naraganset Cuntry in ye Kings province, the governm't whereof is for clearely by his Maj'ts Authority Comited unto us That we dare not in obedience to his Maj'ts declare our duties or suit others to exercise Authoritie in ye Kings province aforesaid, And therefore in obedience to his Maj'ts and in ye execution there of We doe hereby in his Maj'ts name, Charles ye Second King of England, Scotland, ffrance & Ireland & desire & require you & all others by any Authority from Conecticot Collonie derived to desist & not to hould any Courte or any otherwise exercise any Authority in any part of ye Kings province aforesaid until his Maj'ts pleasure be otherwise knowne, And we doe hereby further Certify and assure yo'r Selves & all others yt in obedience to his Maj'ts, We are and shall be ready to p'forme our duties & in order there unto if there be any ocation for ye houlding a Court of Justice or other Exercise of Authority, we shall apply our Selves to afford all lawfull inshare to such p'sons who have just complaint and adress them Selves accordingly.

Signed by order of ye Gen'll Councill of his Maj'ts Collony of Rhoad Island & providence plantations & Siting at mr. Smith's house in Naraganset ye 21 day of August, 1672.

John Sanford, Secritary.

The mesinger demanded an answer to this writeing but ye Court see not any cause to send them any at present, The Court being informed, by ye Constable mr. Eldred, of same contempt yt others had cast upon ye Authority of Conecticot, ordered warant to call them before them.

Copie of ye warant for Steven Northrop, you are hereby required in his Maj'ts name to warne Steven Northrop & him require in his Maj'ts name to appeare forth wth before ye Court now siting by order of ye Collonie of Conecticot at Capt. Hudson's house to Answer for his casting contempt upon his Maj'ts Authority of Conecticot Collony Setled by charter & hereof not to faile upon yo'r perill, dated 22 Aug'st, 1672, by order of ye Court.

Edward Hutchinson, Recorder.

To Samuel Eldred, Constable of Wickford.

The Answer of Steven Northrop when ye Constable Served this warant upon him I denie to obey any warant from ye Authority of Conecticot, If ye governm't of Roade Island send any I will obay them but not this warant nor any from Conecticot Collony.

Capt. Jonathan Atherton upon oath testifies to ye truth of this his answer to the above warant & ye constable also affirmes ye same.

Thomas Nicols also upon oath testifies before ye Court yt Steven Northrop refused to obay ye warant above, 22 August, 1672, Sworne before ye Court by boke.

Edward Hutchinson, Recorder.

(2*) 22 August, 1672.

This morning came Capt. Cranston & ye rest of ye Gentlemen of Roade Island to the Court to Capt. Hudsons & required us not to proceed in o'r Court, and in conclusion read to us, by there secritary, ye declaration formerly mentioned, upon wch we declared to them yt we had sent them, also a declaration agt. there P'seedinge but ye mesinger meeting them by ye way we thought it good now then to delaver it, wch we did & read it alsoe & only before them wch was as followeth.

To Capt. Jo. Cranston and ye rest of ye gentlemen Assembled at mr. Smith's house or any others whome it may concerne, where as Naraganset Countrie is undoubtedly Cercumscribed wth in ye gracious grant of our Lord ye Kinge under ye great seale of England, unto ye Collonie of Conecticot where they have asserted & exerted Governm't for divers yeares past, we by returne of ye said Authoritie doe there fore in his Maj'ts name declare against & prohibit you or any others from exerciseing any power wth in ye Limits of Naraganset where ye Governm't of Conecticot hath exserted Jurisdiction, Except onely such as doe or shall derive Authority from ye Generall Assembly of Conecticot.

Dated 22 August, 1672.
by order of ye Court Edward Hutchinson Recorder.

After this donne this warrant following was served on Tho. Goold.

To mr. Thomas Goold;
you are hereby required in his Maj'ts name to appeare forte wth before ye Court, now siting by order of ye Collonie of Conecticot at Capt. Hudson house, to Answer for yo'r Casting contempt upon his Maj'ts Authoritie here setled by ye generall Assembly of Conecticot, according to his Maj'ts charter & here of you are not to faile upon yo'r perill.

Dated 22 August, 1772.
by order of ye Court Edward Hutchinson, Recorder; Thomas Goold in open Court refused to obay ye warrant above, After

wch Capt. Cranston & Capt. Greene both warned mr. Goold & all others p'sent in his Maj'ts name not to obay yt warant or any other warrants from ye Courte, upon wch answer when they called a Constable apprehended Mary Johnston wch was plantife in ye complaint before mentioned, & carryed her away yt thereby they might abstruct ye Pleading of ye Court, but ye Court declaired ag't them and P'seeded to take the testimony ag't mr. Goold wch is as follows.

At Wickford ye 7 of August, 1672, mr. Thomas Goold answer is That he doth not value ye warneing of mr. Samuel Eldreds warrant to appeare ye 21 August, at ye Comisioners Court at Wickford, & said he did not nor would not yeeld any obedience to any such Comandments, these words above written mr. Thomas Goold did replie as an Answer to mr. Eldreds warant, emediately after ye warant was read to mr· Thomas Goold in his house.

22 August, 1672, Robert Cooke tooke his oath to ye truth of what is above written in open Court ye Constable affirmeing ye same.

sworn in Court Edward Hutchinson, Recorder, this done ye Court desolved.

(3* blank. 4*) Kings Province, June 23th 1686.
At a Court held by his Maj'tes Commission and Justices at Maj'r Richard Smith's in Rochester in ye Kings Province.

Present
    Joseph Dudley, Esq'r, President.
    John Winthrop,   ⎫
    Edward Randolph, ⎬ Esq'rs of his Maj'ties Councill.
    Richard Wharton, ⎭
    John Blackwell,   ⎫
    Elisha Hutchinson, ⎪
    Rich'd Smith,   ⎬ Esq'rs.
    Francis Brinley,   ⎪
    John Saffin,   ⎭

John Fones, }
Thomas Ward, } Gent.
James Pendleton. }

Imprimus, The power and Commission of ye President, and ye rest of ye hono'rd Gentlemen Commissioned for that purpose was Read, and ye President and all ye Justices, there Assembled tooke ye Oath prescribed in said Commission and ye Justices oath, also Capt. John Blackwell, Capt. Elisha Hutchinson, mr. ffrancis Brinley, mr. John Saffin, Esq'rs, and mr. Thomas Ward tooke ye oath of Allegiance — John Fones sworne unto ye office of Clerke to S'd coort and all coorts which shall hereafter be held in ye Kings Province for ye time being — The Kings Commission to ye President & councill of his Territory & Dominion in New England, Openly read — Commissions unto all ye commissioned officers of ye Respective companies of ye Militia in Kings Province Delivered by ye President, they haveing formerly taken oath of allegiance — Ordered that ye three Towns now in ye Kings Province Shall be called Rochester ye first & chiefe formerly called Kingstowne, Feversham ye Second formerly called Westerly, Dedford ye the third formerly Greenwich — Elisha Hutchinson, Esq'r, having Exhibited a Booke and Reference & Report thereon under ye hands of John Pynshon, Bartholomew Gidney & Jonathan Tyng, Esq'rs, and ye order for allowance by ye President & councill at Boston, Dated ye seventeenth of this instant month of June, It is ordered that ye S'd Booke & Report & allowance thereon be committed to Capt. John Fones, Clerke & Recorder of this Province, and that ye matters Entered in ye S'd Booke, Stand & Remaine Authenticke Records of this Province and into ye Same Booke, The Clerke is ordered to Enter Such further Records, grants & Bargaines of land &c. as shall be acknowledged & allowed before ye President or Some member of his Maj'ties councill from time to time under their hands with such other Deeds as have been allowed by former Authoritie — And it is ordered that two coorts of Pleas shall be held yearly at Rochester, The first court to hold ye Second monday in october and ye other ye last monday in may — And for ye Impartiall Issue of Titles of land within this Province, and that absent Claimers may not be impeded nor exception made against ye Judges, Severall of his Maj'ties councill & justices assigned to hold his Maj'ties court, here being convened in ye Generall Titles — It is ordered that all originall writs in Reall actions Shall be served at least thirty dayes before ye session of ye court that shall try ye case, and that declarations be filed in Six daies after ye process is served, and that ye Clerke of ye court for ye time being Shall at least eighteen daies before ye Sessson of ye court Transmit to ye President or Dept. President an Account of all Actions Entered & Depending on ye Gen'll titles — And it is ordered that in all other cases ye proceedings of court in this Province be agreeable to ye Gen'll orders & Directions for Administration of Justice in other parts of his Maj'ties Territory & Dominion und'r this Government — ffor ye Settlements of Precints of Townes and ye Governm't of ye militia — It is ordered that ye Bounds of ye Towne of Rochester in ye Kings Province Shall be accounted to begin at ye Mill River to ye Eastward of James Reynolds, Sen'r, his house and to Extend to ye westermost Bounds of ye tract of land commonly Knowne by ye name of Petiquamscut as it is Bounded by ye agreement made ye twenty fifth of Decemb'r, 1679, including the Northern & Southern tract purchased by ye late John Winthrop, Esq'r, & others also S'd Petiquamscut tract & Inhabitants thereof — It is ordered That ye Bounds of ye Towne of ffeversham in ye Kings Province Shall accounted to begin at Rochester and Extend to pawcatuck River — It is ordered That ye Bounds of ye Towne of Dedford in ye Kigns Province Shall begin at Rochester Bounds and to Extend unto ye Bounds of Warwick, includeing all ye lands in ye Kings Province to ye Eastward of ye S'd Towne of Rochester, (viz.) the lands formerly called East Greenwich, Quoheset & Potowomack and ye Inhabitants thereof — It is ordered That all other Inhabitants in ye Kings Province Shall belong to and attend their Respective duties in Such of ye above S'd Townes as their habitants lye nearest until further orders — for as much as Sundry Persons have been deluded and whilst no Governm't was setled upon ye place have been Encouraged without lycense from ye proprieto'rs to build & make Improvemen'ts upon ye lands called ye Mortgage lands — To ye End therefore that all such persons may have Seasonable time to make their compasitions that so they Either upon Purchase Rents or other good Agreem'ts Enjoy their Respective Improvem'ts where ye same are not predjudiciall to Townships nor highwayes, It is ordered that no possesser as Incombent off or upon, and such lands shall be mollested nor any action upon Title of land brought against them before ye twentieth day of August next, and in case upon Treaty with ye propriet'rs or their committe, they receive not satisfaction in ye Towne, The s'd possesso'rs or Incumbents Shall upon their complaint be heard by ye President & Councill at Boston, (and relieve so farr as may be consistant with common Justice & his Maj'ties Service) who will further direct to ye Tryall & Issue of ye Differences — The court Adjourned till ye next day at Eight of ye clock — June ye 24th, 1686, The s'd court again satt — Ordered that thirty or any less number of wild or unmarked horses to two yeares old or upwards Shall be taken up and by order of two of ye Justices of ye Peace sold and ye produce Imployed for ye building a Prison and Erecting stocks, and that Daniell Vernon be appointed Marshall of ye Province an Prison Keeper — Ordered That Coppies of all publick acts & orders of this court be fairly drawned and sent to ye Constables to be published in ye sevearall Townes in this Province — In Answer to ye complaint of James Coose late Servant to John Carr showing his Indenture & complaining that he is Dismissed after Nine yeares Service by ye s'd Indenture without nescessary Apparall, all which oth appeare unto ye court — It is therefore ordered by ye court that ye s'd John Carr, ye Master, doe provide & Deliver unto ye S'd Servant one suite of Cloaths, one Shirt, Stockings & Shoes meet for Such a Servant for his body, within tenn daies next or pay unto him foure pounds to provide for himselfe — Ordered That foure dayes in ye yeare be appoynted for training, and that ye Penalty for non Appearance be six shillings Eight pence P. head — Ordered That all horse kind that are to be carried or transported out of ye Kings Province shall be viewed & Registerod by ye Clerke before they be carried away out of ye Province although not Entered before —

P. order of Court, John Fones, Clerke & Recorder.

(5*) Kings Province october ye 13th, 1686.

At a Court held for his Majesty in Rochester in ye Kings at ye house of Maj'r Richard Smith.

Present.

John Winthrop, Esq'rs, one of the Councill,

Elisha Hutchinson,
Richard Smith,
Francis Brinley,
John Saffin,
} Esq'rs.

John Fones,
Thomas Ward,
James Pendleton,
} Gent.

The Commission to ye Justices from ye President & Councill for holding ye courts in ye Kings Province was openly read in court — The Petition of mr. Simon Lynde which was Exhibited ye last court here in ye Kings Province, and Referred to this court, no Person appearing to Speake in that behalfe or to manage ye complaint ye s'd Petitioners Suspended, and their being no Action depending nor other Business of Moment The court Disolved.

P. order court, John Fones, Clerke & Recorder.

[THE END.]

Contents.

I

THE COMPANY'S PAPERS.

1	Preamble.	1
1*	Cojinaquands gift of the Northern Tract.	1
2	Cojinaquands gift of the Southern Tract.	1
3	Orders of the Company.	4
4	Ceshequansh and Scuttupo gift of Confirmation.	6
5	Ceshequansh, Cojinaquand and Scuttup's gift of Confirmation.	7
6	Ceshequnosh, Scuttup and Wequachanuit's Confirmation.	8
7	Quequachanuits Confirmation.	9
8	Suckquansh, Nenograt, Scuttup and Wequachanuit's Confirmation.	10
8*	Names of the Company with agreement about taking possession.	12
9	The Sachems Receipt.	14
10	John Winthrop's Receipt.	15
11	Tumteckowe's deed.	15
12	Orders of the Company.	17
13	Doings of Company's Committee.	18
14	Orders of the Company.	19
15	" " " "	21
16	" " " "	21
17	" " " "	23
17*	" to Mr. Richison.	24
18	Petition to Connecticutt.	24

19	Orders Concerning the Southern Tract.	25
19*	Orders concerning both the Northern and Southern Tract.	27
20	Orders of the Company	29
21	" " " "	30
22	" " " "	31
23	" " " "	32
24	Agreement with the Pettequamscutt Company.	33
24*	Farms laid out, their size and to whom sold.	36
25	Doings of the Company's Committee.	37
26	Committee Appointed.	39
27	Orders concerning the Southern Tract.	40
28	Deed, Edward Hutchinson to Elisha Hutchinson.	42
29	Deed, Jonathan Atherton, Adm. to Thomas Deane and John Saffin.	45
30	Deed, Jonathan Atherton, Adm. to John Saffin.	47
31	Doings of Company's Committee.	49
31*	Confirmation of the Records.	50

II

THE FONES RECORD.

1	Orders for Committee.	52
2	The Kings Commission.	53
3	The Councils Commission.	59
4	The Councils Report to the King.	64
5	Deed of Exchange between Francis Brinley and Samuel Viall.	75
6	Deed, Randall Holden to William Taylor and Richard Wharton.	77
7	Deed, William Mayes to William Taylor and Richard Wharton.	79
8	Deed, Samuel Cranston and Mary Jones to Richard Smith.	81
9	James Russell, Exc. to Richard Wharton.	83

10	Deed, Richard Smith to Richard Wharton.	85
11	Deed, Henry Fowler to Thomas Clarke.	87
12	Deed, Capt. Thomas Clarke to Capt. William Hudson.	89
13	Deed, Capt. William Hudson to Henry Tibbetts.	91
14	Deed, Roger Williams to Richard Smith.	93
15	Lease, Tasaquanat alias Coginaquand to Richard Smith.	94
16	Lease, Coginaquand to Richard Smith, Sr. and Richard Smith, Jr.	97
17	Coginaquand's grant of a small island to Richard Smith, Jr.	99
18	Scuttube and Quequaganewett confirmation to Richard Smith.	100
19	Deed, Capt. William Hudson to Richard Smith.	103
20	Deed, William Maze to Richard Smith.	104
21	Deed, Randall Holden to Richard Smith.	106
22	Agreement between Richard Wharton and Thomas Mumford.	109
23	Deed, Samuel Cranston and Mrs. Mary Jones to Richard Smith.	110
24	Deed, John Vyall to Richard Smith.	112
25	Deed, Capt. Jonathan Atherton to Richard Smith.	115
26	Deed, Richard Smith to Francis Brinley.	116
27	Deed, Richard Smith to Francis Brinley.	117
28	Deed, Thomas Newton to Francis Brinley.	118
29	Atherton's Confirmation to Richard Smith.	120
30	Deed, Jonathan Atherton to Richard Smith.	122
31	Deed, Richard Smith to Francis Brinley.	125
32	Deed, Jonathan Atherton to Francis Brinley.	128
33	Deed, Richard Updike to Francis Brinley.	130
34	Deed, Atherton's Confirmation deed to Richard Smith.	132
35	Richard Smith quit claim deed to John Fones.	134
36	John Winthrop's Confirmation to Richard Dummer.	135
37	Deed, Richard Dummer to Jeremiah Dummer.	137

38	Deed, Jeremiah Dummer to John Fones.	138
39	Deed, Joshua Hews to John Fones.	140
40	Alice Hews quit claim to John Fones.	143
41	Deed, George Denison to Symon Lynde.	144
42	Deed, Daniel Gookin to Symon Lynde.	147
43	Deed, Amos Richardson to Symon Lynde.	149
44	Deed Stephen Richardson to Symon Lynde.	151
45	Deed, Thomas Bell to Symon Lynde.	153
46	Amos Richardson's letter to Symon Lynde.	155
47	Deed, Richard Smith to John Briggs.	156
48	Deed, Richard Smith to William Palmer.	157
49	Deed, Samuell Wilson to Henry Bull.	159
50	Agreement to build a Grist and Fulling mill on Mattatuxet river.	161
51	Deed, James Updike to Francis Brinley.	162
52	Receipt to Richard Wharton.	164
53	Acknowledgement of Receipt.	165
54	Deed, Anashuecott and others to John Fones & others.	166
55	Account of Disbursements.	170
56	A Commissioners Court at Wickford.	172

General Index.

A

Absolome 167, 168, 169
Acre price per acre 5, 17, 18, 27
Adderton Maj. Humphrey, (see Atherton) 6, 7, 8
Aderton, Maj. Humphrey, (see Atherton) 1, 4, 5, 10, 11 13
Addington Isaac 47, 146
Agreements to be recorded 29, 30
Akins widow 36
Alcock Dr. John 13, 19, 20, 23, 30, 31, 38, 39, 40, 170, 171
Allyn John 12, 64, 65, 96, 99, 100, 102, 146, 149
Allegiance oath of 58, 63
Alsbrough Capt. 37
Anashuecot or Anashuecot 167, 168, 169
Ancient Grant 69
Ancient Inhabitants 66, 68
Andrews John 165, 167, 168
Arnold Asa 164
Arnold Josiah 34, 36, 37
Atherton Consider 121, 122
Atherton Hope 121, 122
Atherton Major Humphrey 1, 2, 3, 4, 5, 12, 13, 15, 16, 17, 19, 20, 21, 22, 26, 31, 32, 33, 34, 35, 36, 37, 38, 39, 40, 41, 45, 47, 49, 51, 65, 70, 71, 72, 73, 113, 121, 122, 127, 128, 132, 134, 164, 165, 171
Atherton Increase 13, 19, 25, 39, 47, 49
Atherton Jacovus 22, 23
Atherton Capt. Jonathan 45, 46, 47, 115, 117, 120, 121, 122, 123, 124, 128, 132, 134, 135, 164, 165, 173
Atherton Patience 127
Atherton Watching 121, 122
Attachments 24
Awashous 15, 16, 98
Awafhus 9
Ayres William 37

B

Beach the 155
Bell Thomas 153, 154, 155
Bendall Grace 149
Bird Thomas 133, 165
Blacksmith 89
Blackwell John 59, 60, 62, 63, 175, 176
Bradstreet Dudley 53, 54
Bradstreet Simon 12, 19, 20, 22, 30, 31, 32, 33, 39, 40, 53, 24, 138
Brenton Frances 31
Brewstert Mr. 15

Briggs John   116, 156, 166, 167, 168
Brinley Frances   37, 38, 59, 60, 63, 75, 76, 77, 81, 82, 86, 106, 111, 116, 117, 119, 120, 122, 124, 125, 126, 128, 129, 130, 131, 133, 134, 162, 163, 174, 175, 176, 179
Brinley William   164
Brooks Thomas   77, 80, 82, 110
Browne   20, 21, 169. 170
Browne James   25, 29, 33
Browne Capt. John   52
Browne John Sr.   6, 13
Browne John   14, 22
Browne J.   19
Bulkley Peter   53, 54
Bull Henry   159, 160
Bull Jerah   35, 36, 118, 139, 143
Bundy William   36
Burden Elizabeth   118, 131
Button John   71

C

Carpenter William 89, 96, 102
Carr Caleb   8, 18, 87, 92
Carr John   104, 178, 179
Casey Michael   37
Case Joseph   112
Ceshequansh   6, 7, 8
Champernoone Frances   54
Champlain Jeffere   94
Chancery Court of   53, 55
Charles II.   36, 47, 49, 87, 91, 92, 103, 115, 117, 124, 126, 131, 134, 136, 139, 142, 146, 149, 151, 152, 163, 166, 172
Charles Capt. Will   27

Charter the   67
Cheffinch Thomas   73
Chief Sachems   18
Clarke John   68, 133, 165
Clarke Thomas   87, 88, 89, 90, 91, 92, 155
Clarke Walter   129
Clarke Weston   127
Coddington Ann   126
Coddington John   126
Coddington Thomas   108
Coddington William   66, 124, 127
Codner George   116
Coggeshall James   160
Coggeshall John   129
Coginaquand   2, 3, 4, 6, 7, 8, 70, 77, 79, 94, 95, 96
Coginaquon   1, 2
Coginiquand   95, 96, 97, 98, 99, 100, 104, 106
Cogiquand   9, 96
Cogiquant   82
Cojanaquant   34, 35
Cojiquant   111
Cojuaquand   40
Cole John   25, 43, 104
College Land   144
Commissioners   10, 12, 13, 14, 15
Commissioners Address   20
Commissioners Court   172
Commissioners His Majesties 38, 68
Committee   18, 20
Common Land   136, 138, 156
Concessions   91
Confirmation the kings   38
Congdon Ben   37
Connecticut agents   38
Cononicus subjection of   66

187

Conscience Liberty of 57
Constables 24
Contempts 63
Controversies 68, 69
Cooke Thomas 175
Cooper a 130
Coose James 178, 179
Cordwainer 140
Cosons Edward 172
Costing William 115, 117
Coston William 160
Cotton William 71
Council His Majesties 50
Council the Priv'y 53
Council oath of 54, 56
Country road 141
Court of Civil and Criminal practice 55, 56
Court General 147, 148
Court ordered 177
Court of Record 55, 56
Crabtree John 25
Craft George 123, 125
Crandall John 80, 104
Cranfield Edward 64, 74, 75
Cranston Major John 9, 15, 16, 18, 27, 82, 110, 174, 175
Cranston Samuel 81, 82, 110, 111, 112
Crossman John 36, 37
Culpeper Lord 38
Cuniegrande Mr. 18
Current money 109

D

Dam to be built 86
Danforth Thomas 149
Deane Thomas 30, 31, 38, 39, 45, 46
Denison Anne 144, 145, 146
Denison Major Daniel 12, 19, 20, 22, 30, 31, 33, 138, 146
Denison Capt George 10, 12, 19, 20, 22, 25, 30, 33, 38, 39, 144, 145, 146, 171
Dexter John 36, 37
Dinners 15
Disorders 24
Dividends 30
Downing William 168
Dry Cattle 23
Dudley Joseph 53, 54, 59, 60, 62 63, 64, 75, 79, 81, 83, 111, 130, 143, 175
Dummer Anna 139, 140
Dummer Jeremiah 137, 138, 139, 140
Dummer Richard 135, 136, 137, 138
Dummer Richard Jr. 138
Dyre Samuel 42, 43, 115, 117, 134

E

Eldred Daniel 42
Eldred Samuel Sr. 28, 41
Eldred Samuel Jr. 25, 41
Eldred Samuel 14, 25, 93, 110, 173, 175
Elliott Asap 42
Endicott Gov. John 71
England Church of 58
Englishmen 1, 3, 99
English Money 122, 125
English 66, 68, 79, 71, 169
Evidences 30

F

Farishee John 4
Farms 22, 23
Fenich Alexander 25
Fishing 156
Fitch John 150

Fones John 52, 59, 60, 75, 77, 79, 81, 85, 87, 89, 91, 93, 94, 97, 99, 100, 103, 104, 106, 108, 110, 112, 115, 116, 118, 120, 122, 125, 127, 128, 129, 130, 131, 132, 133, 134, 135, 136, 138, 139, 140, 141, 142, 143, 144, 146, 149, 151, 153, 155, 157, 159, 161, 162, 164, 165, 166, 167, 168, 169, 176, 177, 179
Fowler Henry 27, 87, 88, 89, 92
Fowler Rebecca 88, 89
Freeke John 133
Frink John 150, 152, 153
Fulling mill 161

G

Goddington Thomas 78
Gallup John 155, 156
Gardiner Ben 37
Gardiner George 37
Garrett Elizabeth 124
Garrett Harmon 72
Gedney Bartholomew 50, 51, 53, 54, 176
General Assembly of Conn, 174
General Assembly of R. I. 66
General Council 173
General Court 144
General Titles 177
Giddeon 10
Gideon 9, 145
Gidley Henry 136
Goates 93
Goldsmith 138
Gold Thomas 87
Gookin Daniel 95, 96, 98, 102, 147, 148, 149
Gookin Mary 147, 148, 149
Goold Thomas 173, 175
Gore John 41, 42, 85
Gorton Benjamin 78, 108
Gorton Samuel 77, 78, 79, 80, 82, 104, 105, 106, 107, 108, 111
Gould John 18, 166
Gould Thomas 18, 23, 27, 92
Greene Henry 168
Greene John 18, 23, 25, 65, 66, 122, 157, 166, 167, 168, 175
Greene Nathaniel 4
Greene Robert 77, 80, 83
Greene Samuel 149
Grist mill 161
Grover Simon 81, 106
Gunsmith 157

H

Hamilton Duke of 74
Hart Thomas 37
Harris William 31, 89. 96, 99, 102, 170
Harvard College grant 69
Haveland Mr. 36
Hewes Joshua 25
Hugehews Mr. 155
Hayward John 49, 115
Hazard Robert 37, 75, 76, 81, 106
Hefferland William 37
Helme Rouse 37
Hewes Alice 143, 144
Hewes Hannah 140, 141, 142, 143
Highways 26, 37, 42, 136, 141, 159
Hinckes John 54
Hinckley Sir Thomas 64, 65

Hixe Susanna	156		171, 176
Hixe William	156	Hutchinson William	45, 84
Holden Frances	79, 108	**I**	
Holden Capt. Randall 3, 65, 66, 77, 78, 79, 82, 104, 105, 106, 107 108, 111		Indian Planting	95
		Indian Royalties	13
		Indian Territory	69
Holmes William	94	Indian War	72
Honeysuckle a red	97	Indians	66, 68, 71
Hooper Christian	10	Infidels	63
Horses	179	Inhabitants	5, 17
Horton Thomas	13	Iron Guns	93
Houses to be built	22	Islands the little	93
House Walter	25	**J**	
Howard John Sir	143	James II 53, 84, 158, 160, 161	
Howard Robert 96, 98, 102, 136			
		James Will	37
Howler Mr.	18	Johnson Hannah	154
Hudson Capt. William 1, 2, 3, 4, 5, 8, 9, 12, 13, 15, 16, 19, 20, 21, 22, 24, 26, 27, 29, 30, 31, 33, 40, 43, 71, 83, 84, 90, 91, 92, 93, 103, 171, 172, 173, 174		Johnson John	172
		Johnson Mary	175
		John	11
		Jones Mary	82, 111, 112
		K	
		Kelland Thomas	49
Huling Alexander	42	Kings Letter Patent	67
Huling Elizabeth	76	Kings Warrant	59
Hull Capt. John 33, 34, 35, 36, 37, 38		Knowles Henry	37
		L	
Hutchinson Capt. Edward 4, 5, 7, 8, 9, 12, 13, 15, 16, 17, 19, 20, 21, 22, 23, 24, 25, 26. 27, 28, 29, 31, 38, 39, 41, 42, 43, 44, 45, 71, 135, 138, 171, 172, 173, 174, 175, 176		Lamb Joshua	33, 38
		Lamb Josioh	65
		Leach Ambros	25, 36, 71
		Leverett Gov. John	47, 133
		Lord Capt, Richard 12, 19, 20, 22, 25, 171	
		Low Mr.	36
Hutchinson Edward Jr. 19, 20		Lynde Simon 30, 31, 33, 38, 39, 40, 64, 65, 69, 73, 144, 145, 147, 148, 149; 150, 151, 152, 153, 154, 155, 179	
Hutchinson Capt. Elisha 12, 23, 24, 28, 30, 31, 32, 34, 36, 37, 38, 39, 40, 42, 43, 44, 50, 52, 59, 60, 62. 63, 65, 73, 85, 86, 114, 170,			
		M	
		Maple Tree	97. 100

Marshall Thomas	160	Nammeash	166, 167, 168
Marsh John	154, 155	Narragansett Court	172
Marsh Mary	155, 156	Narragansett Sachems	1, 3, 6, 7, 9
Martine John	104		
Mason Robert	53, 54	Narragansett settlement	72
Mather Timothy	22, 25, 127	Narragansetts	69
Mattaickis	56	Newbury plantation	35
Mayes Sarah	81, 108	Newcombe	9
Mayes William	80, 81, 104, 105, 106	Newcom	14
		New England Money	83, 87, 90, 112, 119, 121, 123, 125, 130, 138, 140, 143, 149, 157, 159, 162
Mead Samuel	161, 162		
Mexcon	100		
Michellson Edward	149		
Militia	57, 62, 177	Neneglad	14, 15
Mill to be built	85	Nenegratt	144
Mill farm for	37	Nenigrat	13, 35
Mill dam	109	Nrnograt	10, 12
Mill Pond	85	Newton Abigail	159
Mill Site	109	Newton Thomas	94, 118, 119 120
Minister a	5		
Ministry farm for the	37	Nickols Col.	68
Miner Ephraim	152, 153	Nickols Thomas	27, 173
Miner Thomas	9, 151, 153, 155	Ninagrautt	70, 71
		Ninicraft	15
Mixon's sons	100	Ninigratt	72
Money to be Advanced	38	Ninigrat	20
Money of New England	38	Northern Tract	5, 17, 18
Monks George	38	Northup Stephen	36, 173
Moody Eleazer	143	Noyes James	73
More Ephraim	162	O	
Mortgages the	35, 39	Oliver Capt. James	103
Mortgage Lands	14, 15, 32, 34, 38, 45, 48, 49, 52, 128, 170, 178	Oliver Edmund	124
		Ompamiatt	166, 167, 168
		Opdyck Gysbert	98, 99
Moseupp	168	Osbond Nathaniel	160
Mosip	111	P	
Mossip	77, 79, 104, 106	Page Nicolas	146
Mumford Peleg	161, 162	Palmer Bethia	161
Mumford Thomas	109, 110, 161, 162	Palmer Edward	59, 60, 62, 63, 64
N		Palmer George	25, 161

Palmer William 157, 158
Palmitter John 89
Panatuk 7, 11
Parkman Elias 170
Park Deacon 156
Pattent the 68
Peague 9, 18, 70
Pearce William Sr. 91
Pendleton James 59, 60, 176, 179
Pequods the 67
Persons deluded 168
Peter 168
Petition to Conn. 24
Pinder Jacob 85, 86
Pissicus 66, 111
Plais Enock 25
Plantation settlement of 18
Ptimouth Charter 69
Plimouth Council 69
Pilmouth Pattent 69, 70
Pole John 47
Powetuck 101
Pratt Samuel 134
Prentice Capt. Thomas 143, 147
Prentis John 164
Prison ordered 178
Proclammation a 65
Profanities 24
Property a pretended 69
Proprietors Book 172
Public acts 178
Purchasers claims 72
Pynchon John 45, 50, 51, 53, 54, 64, 74, 176

Q
Quequacknuit 9
Quequaganuett 70, 100, 101, 102
Quequashanuit 9
Quescoquons 14, 12

R
Randolph Edward 51, 54, 59, 60, 63, 64, 74, 164, 175
Rawson Edward 9
Real actions 177
Record book 29
Remedy for wrongs 178
Reynolds James 177
Reynolds John 14ĩ
Rhodes John 71
Rhode Islanders 68, 72
Rhode Island a committee from 32
Richardson Amos 5, 29, 33, 103, 136, 138, 149, 150, 151, 153, 156, 170, 171
Richardson Lydia 151, 152
Richardson Mary 150, 151
Richardson Stephen 151, 152
Richardson Amos 1, 2, 3, 5
Richieson Amos 15, 16
Richeson Amos 6, 8, 12, 14, 17, 21, 22, 23, 25, 26, 28, 29, 31
Richeson Amos 3, 5, 19, 20, 40
Richison Mr. 24
Robert 10
Roome John 94
Royal Letter 71
Russell James 83, 84, 85
Russell John 38
Russell Richard 83, 84

S
Sachems the 33, 34; 35, 40, 45, 48, 67, 68, 70, 72, 77, 79, 93, 94, 97, 99, 100, 101, 104, 105, 106, 107, 111, 145, 169
Saffin John 26, 29, 30, 31, 32, 34, 36, 37, 39, 40, 42, 45, 46, 47, 49, 52, 59, 60,

63, 64, 65, 73, 85, 86, 110, 170, 174, 175, 176, 179
Saggamor's the 71
Sails John 18
Saltonstall Edward 64
Saltonstall Nathaniel 53, 54, 74
Sanford John 15, 16, 18, 19, 125, 157, 173
Sanford Major Peleg 34, 36, 37, 169
Sassaman John 7
Savage Thomas 144
Sayles John 89
Seire Feacias 53
Scuthop 12
Scuttape 15
Scuttop 5, 7, 13
Scuttube 100, 101, 102
Scuituop 144
Scuttup 6, 7, 8, 9, 10, 11, 70, 71
Seal of England 174
Seawell Capt. Samuel 159
Seecomp 166, 167, 168
Sequenck 70
Sergeant General 65
Sewall Samuell 38, 59, 60, 62, 63
Sewall 25, 93
Sheldon John 161, 162
Sherman Eber 37
Sherman Edward 37
Sherman Sampson 37
Shipwright 162
Shrimpton Samuel 64, 74
Smith Esther 157, 158, 159
Smith Hester 86, 98, 99
Smith James 2, 3, 12, 13, 16, 19, 20, 39, 98
Smith Richard 1, 2, 3, 4, 5, 8, 12, 13, 14, 16, 18, 19,
20, 23, 24, 25, 26, 27, 28, 29, 31, 36, 38, 39, 40, 41, 42, 50, 59, 60, 62, 63, 64, 73, 77, 79, 80, 82, 83, 85, 86, 87, 93, 94, 95, 96, 97, 99, 100, 101, 102, 105, 107, 110, 111, 112, 113, 114, 115, 116, 117, 118, 119, 120, 121, 122, 123, 124, 125, 126, 127, 128, 130, 132, 133, 135, 139, 140, 141, 156, 157, 158, 159, 161, 162, 163, 164, 174, 175, 179
Smith Major Richard 1, 2, 3, 4, 5, 8, 12, 13, 16, 17, 20, 21, 23, 25, 32, 34, 37, 39, 52, 71, 94, 95, 96, 97, 99, 100, 101, 102, 103, 109, 131, 142, 170, 171
Smith Weston 2, 17
Snooke John 113
Southern Tract 5, 17
Sobkquansh 9, 13
Speare Richard 42
Spink Robert 27, 115, 117, 141
Stanton Daniel 169
Stanton John 4, 151, 153, 155
Stanton Robert 153
Stanton Thomas Sr. 4, 10, 12, 19, 20, 22, 25, 30, 147, 148, 171
Stanton Thomas Jr. 12, 19, 20, 22, 25
Steavens Hen 25
Stephens Walter Jr. 82, 111
Sterling money 144, 147
Stoughton William 53, 54, 59, 60, 62, 63, 64, 74, 75
Strange Lieut. 81, 106, 129

Suckquansh 10, 11, 144
Sweet James 118
Sweet John 14
Swift Obadiah 133, 165
Sylvester G. 76
Sylvester Joseph 131

T
Tailor 153
Tanner William 79, 108
Tasaquanatt 95
Tasaquanet 95, 111
Tasaquonet 82
Tasaquonett 96
Tasiquonitt 96
Taxes 58
Taylor Robert 120
Taylor William 31, 33, 37, 38, 39, 77, 78, 79, 80, 81, 104, 105, 106, 107, 165, 170
Teeppetts Henry 157
Thomas John 115
Thomas Capt. Nathaniel 52
Tibbitts Hen 27, 91, 92
Tib't Henry 25
Tidgett Charles 165
Tift John 37
Tinker John 1, 2, 3, 4, 5, 26, 31, 40
Tocomminon 169
Tocomino 6
Torry Joseph 89, 91, 93
Township set up 23
Town bounds 177
Town mens 176
Trading House 93, 97, 99, 100, 130, 162
Trott Bernard 47
Trowbridge James 127
Tumteckowe 15, 16
Turf and Twigg 71
Tybits Henry 166, 167, 168
Tyecueesha 166, 167, 168
Tyng Edward 49, 54, 140
Tyng Jonathan 50, 51, 53, 54, 176

U
United Colonies 67
Updike James 162, 163, 164
Updike Lodowick 110, 127, 159
Updike Richard 116, 124, 130, 131, 133
Usher John 45, 53, 54, 118

V
Vernon Daniel 178
Viall John 4, 29, 31, 33, 91, 103, 134, 170
Viall Samuel 75, 76
Vintner 90, 103
Virtue to be protected 37
Vice to be punished 57
Vyall Elizabeth 112, 113, 114
Vyall John 112, 113, 114, 115, 117

W
Wadsworth John 64, 65
Waite Samuel 25, 95, 96, 101, 102, 156
Wampkegge 166, 167
Wampom 10, 14, 15
Wanamachan 35
Ward Thomas 59, 60, 176, 179
Warren Humphrey 49
Washaucutt 169
Waterman Thomas 27, 166, 167, 168
Webitamuck 15
Welles Peter 79, 108, 135
Wequachunuit 8, 9, 10
Wequnkunuit 11, 12, 144
West Francis 120

Wharton Richard 31, 32, 33, 37, 38, 39, 40, 42, 52, 53, 54, 59, 60, 65, 66, 73, 77, 78, 79, 80, 81, 82, 83, 84, 85, 86, 89, 91, 94, 96, 98, 99, 100, 102, 104, 105, 106, 107, 108, 109, 110, 112, 116, 120, 122, 127, 135, 157, 164, 165, 170, 175
Wharton William 39, 66
Wharves 26
Whipple John Jr. 36, 37
Whitman Valentine 7, 8, 9, 11, 18
Wickes Joseph 121, 122
Wightman George 122, 168
Wilbour Samuel 21, 33, 34, 35, 36
Wilcox Capt. 23
Wilderness the 144, 147, 148
Willett Capt. Thomas 5, 6, 12, 13, 15, 16, 17, 19, 20, 26, 30, 31, 39
Williams John 30, 31, 129, 170
Williams Roger 93, 94

Willis Ruben 2, 11, 16, 25, 95, 96, 98, 101, 102, 156
Willis Samuel 172
Willson Samuel 159, 160
Wilson John 146
Winthrop Major Elisha 39
Winthrop Fitz John 54, 64
Winthrop Gov. John 1, 2, 3, 4, 5, 6, 8, 12, 15, 16, 19, 20, 22, 26, 29, 31, 33, 34, 35, 39, 40, 42, 51, 59, 60, 62, 63, 65, 68, 69, 70, 71, 72, 73, 81, 115, 117, 132, 133, 135, 136, 137, 139, 146, 149, 171, 175, 177, 179
Winthrop Capt. Waite 22, 25, 30, 31, 33, 38, 39, 40, 53, 54, 64, 65, 85, 132, 133, 170, 171
Winslow Major Josias 5, 6, 12, 14, 19, 20, 23, 39, 103
Withington William 41
Woodcock's meeting at 170
Woodmansey John 4
Writings to be recorded 30

Index to Places.

A
Acquidnesset 134
America 53, 59, 83, 85, 116, 122
Anachutuckett river 97
Anachutuck river. 80
Annaquatuckett river 79, 80
Annogatucket river 41, 85, 86
Annoxett Island 82
Annocktusick river 79
Anochetuckett river 3, 94, 101
Anochetucket 3
Anocketucket river 110
Anocotuckett 104, 106
Anoquatuckett river 158
Aquidnessett 132

B
Barbadoes isles 157
Bay the main 94
Boston Neck 25, 26, 28, 29, 43, 75, 76, 109, 112, 119, 121, 123, 125, 127, 132
Boston Mass. 1, 3, 12, 15, 17, 29, 30, 31, 32, 38, 39, 40, 41, 42, 45, 47, 49, 51, 54, 61, 66, 74, 79, 82, 83, 85, 87, 89, 90, 91, 92, 103, 104, 106, 109, 118, 129, 131, 132, 133, 134, 138, 140, 143, 144, 147, 148, 149, 151, 153, 162, 164, 165, 176

C
Cambridge Mass. 147
Charleston Mass 83
Cocumcosutt Harbor 97, 99
Cocumcosutt 97, 99, 100
Cocumcrosuck River 2
Cocumcrosuck 1, 2, 3
Cocumcroset river 3
Cocumscrusuck 2
Cocumsesset 3
Cocumsessuck brooke 40
Cocumsessuck 40
Common path 103, 107
Connecticut Colony 24, 64, 73, 75, 96, 99, 100, 102, 128, 132, 135, 139, 146, 149, 172, 173, 174
Connecticut (spelled variously) 1, 3, 8, 12, 14, 15, 23, 24, 30, 33, 40, 67, 68, 69, 71, 170, 171, 173, 174
Connonacutt 140
Cononicott 138
Coweset Country 10, 33, 35, 144, 145
Cowhesett Country 69, 70
Crab Rock 28

D
Dedford 176, 177
Dorchester Mass. 1, 13, 15, 33, 45, 47, 115, 122, 128
Devils foot 166

E

East Greenwich 177
England 38, 53, 55, 61, 87, 92, 93, 118, 124, 126, 131, 139, 142, 156, 158, 161, 163, 172, 174
English path 18, 94, 100
English 7, 15
Essex Co. Mass. 137

F

Feversham, R. I. 176, 177
Fox Island 77, 79, 80, 82, 104, 105, 106, 107
France 53, 87, 92, 93, 118, 124, 126, 131, 158, 160, 163, 166, 172

G

Great Britain 160, 166
Greenwich, R. I. 176

H

Hartford, Ct. 12, 71, 120
Harvard College 69
Homogansett 77, 79, 82, 104, 105, 106, 107

I

Indians 7, 8
Ipswich, Mass. 12
Island the little 99, 100, 104, 106
Ireland 53, 87, 92, 93, 118, 124, 126, 131, 158, 160, 163, 166, 172

J

Jamestown, R. I. 138, 140, 143
Judea Point 15

K

Kesecomoek 110
Kesicomucke 106
Kesicomuck 104
Kesoconico 82

Kings Province 51, 52, 53, 60, 63, 64, 65, 74, 75, 82, 85, 109, 110, 112, 116, 117, 122, 123, 125, 127, 129, 130, 131, 132, 133, 156, 159, 161, 164, 166, 172, 175, 176, 177, 178, 179
Kings Towne 77, 176

L

Little Creek 28
London, Eng. 31, 84

M

Maine 53
Manhegan 15
Marshfield, Mass. 12
Mascacorwage 2
Mascackawage river 2
Mascuchawage 2
Maskchechuaug river 166
Masquechwaug river 169
Massachusetts Bay 53, 55
Massachusetts Colony 42, 89, 98, 102, 122, 135, 136, 138, 140, 144
Massachusetts Plantation 67
Massachusetts 1, 3, 8, 40, 71, 95, 98, 102
Matutucket river 40, 41
Mattatuxett river 161
Mattatuxett 109
Mattatuxet river 34
Mattatuxset 3
Mattutuxsett river 3
Mill Pond 26, 28
Mill River 177
Musquatek 144

N

Namecock Neck 3, 21, 41
Namecock 70
Namocock Neck 6
Namocock 97, 101

Nanaquaesett 106
Nanaquakesett 109
Nanaquaxett 82, 114
Nanequassett 77, 79
Narragansett Bay 67, 69, 70, 73, 87, 92
Narragansett Country 10, 18, 21, 22, 29, 30, 31, 32, 33, 35, 40, 42, 43, 45, 48, 49, 51, 53, 60, 64, 65, 67, 68, 69, 70, 71, 72, 73, 74, 75, 77, 79, 83, 87, 90, 94, 100, 103, 104, 106, 119, 121, 123, 125, 128, 130, 132, 135, 137, 138, 140, 144, 145, 156, 161, 162, 164, 166, 172, 174
Naragansett Lands 19, 40
Narragansett River 67, 69. 79, 73
Narragansett 1, 3, 7, 8, 9, 10, 12, 14, 15, 16, 17, 18, 20, 23, 24, 25, 27, 28, 29, 31, 38, 50, 69, 79, 85, 91, 93, 97, 99, 103, 105, 107, 110, 112, 115, 117, 118, 119, 121, 123, 125, 127, 128, 130, 132, 134, 139, 142, 145, 156, 164, 166, 170, 173, 174
Nashua 1, 3, 40
Neaticott Country 10, 144, 145
Neck purchase 40
Newbury, Mass. 135, 137
Newbury Plantation 35
Newbury 77
New England Province 151
New England Territory 157
New England 42, 45, 47, 48, 53, 54, 57, 58, 59, 61. 67, 75, 83, 85, 87, 89, 90, 91, 98, 102, 103, 104, 106, 112, 116, 122, 131, 133, 135, 136, 137, 138, 139, 140, 143, 147, 151, 157, 159, 161, 164, 165, 166, 176
New Hampshire 53, 64
New London, Conn. 110, 144, 166
Newport, R. I. 75, 80, 81, 93, 104, 110, 116, 117, 119, 125, 127, 128, 130, 162, 168
New Plimouth Colony 112
New Plimouth 64
Niantick Country 21, 22, 29, 32, 33, 35, 69, 70, 72
Nipmug Country 69
Nonoquassett 105, 107
Northern Purchase 115, 121, 134, 156
Northern Tract 5, 6, 27, 31, 70, 171, 177
North Tract 170
Northwest Line 34

P

Paquinapange 97
Pasacaco Pond 41
Pusutat 166
Pawtucket Country 69
Patuckett River 69, 70
Pausacaco 34
Pawcuckaron Pond 3
Pawcuckaron 3
Pawcatuck River 147, 148, 177
Pawcatuck Neck 150, 151, 153
Pawquatuck River 67, 69, 70, 73

Pawquatuck	68
Petaquamscott	71
Petaquamscott	32
Petaquamscott	3
Petequamscott	32
Petequamscot River	34, 40
Petequamscot	22
Pettequamscutt Harbour	121, 123, 125
Petiquamscot	177
Petyquamscott Land	38
Pittewomuck River	87, 94
Pequod Country	68, 69, 73, 144, 147
Pittaquamscutt Harbour	123
Pitt Comicutt Harbour	16
Plymouth Colony	69, 70
Plimouth	69, 71
Point Juda Neck	16, 22, 23, 34, 128
Pond the great	15
Poquitt	94
Portsmouth	93
Potomcasutt	94
Potomcasutt Harbour	94
Potoume River	1
Potowomuck River	92
Potowomuck	2, 177
Providence Plantations	69, 104, 106, 140, 143
Providence	37, 69, 73, 87, 89, 93

Q

Quakesett	166
Quckeset	166
Quenaniquatt	134
Quenebang Country	69
Quoheset	177
Quononaqutt	166

R

Rehobath Mass.	12, 69
Rhode Island Colony	89, 92, 93, 138, 149, 143, 166
Rhode Island and Providence Plantations	65, 89, 124, 157, 161, 166, 173
Rhode Islend Plantatlons	67
Rhode Islanders	73
Rhode Island	15, 17, 23, 66, 67, 68, 69, 72, 75, 80, 81, 93, 104, 117, 125, 128, 130, 162, 168, 172, 173, 174
Rhode Isle	32
Road the common	94
Rochester R. I.	52, 79, 81, 89, 91, 93, 94, 96, 98, 99, 100, 104, 106, 108, 109, 112, 116, 120, 122, 127, 129, 131, 132, 133, 135, 157, 158, 159, 161, 175, 176, 177, 179
Rocky Hill	97
Roxbury Mass.	13

S

Sachames the	2. 3, 6, 7, 8, 10, 14, 15,
Sagamores the	6, 7, 8, 9
Sawanoxott Island	77, 79
Sawgoe	97
Scotland	53, 87, 92, 93, 118, 124, 126, 131, 158, 163, 172
Seakunke Mass.	6, 13
Shawatuckquese river	97
Shewotuck Creeke	101
Shewatucket	104 106 107 110
Smith's trading house	5
Southern Purchase	112, 113
Southern Tract	6, 25, 26, 27, 28, 31, 40, 70, 171, 177
Southertown Ct,	12

South Sea	67
South Tract	170
Sowanoxett	104, 105, 106
Squamacock Neck	150, 151, 153
Stonington, Ct.	141, 144, 150, 151, 152, 153, 155, 171
Stony River	18
Suffolk Co. Mass.	87
Sugar Loaf Hill	26, 29
Swansey, Mass.	75, 112

T

Taunton, Mass.	37
Trading house	9

U

United Colonies	10, 14, 24

W

Wackquage	127
Wannalchercomoscut	3
Wannamoqutt	15
Wannuchecomscut	3
Warwick, R. I.	73, 77, 79, 104, 106, 111, 161, 177
Wash Quauge	112
Waters the broad	94
Wenannateke	15
Wecapaug Brook	68, 69
Wecapaug River	73
Weequapaug Brook	144
Wequapaug Neck	144
Westerly, R. I.	176
West line	34
Westminster, Eng.	59, 67
Weyanicock	16
Whiteholl, Eng,	64, 66
Wickford, R. I.	71, 134, 156, 172, 173, 175
Wyapumscut	2

www.ingramcontent.com/pod-product-compliance
Lightning Source LLC
Chambersburg PA
CBHW070742160426
43192CB00009B/1543